Land a Federal Job with the
Successful Outline Format Federal Resume

Jobseeker's Guide

Ten Steps to a Federal Job® for Military and Spouses

7th EDITION
KATHRYN TROUTMAN
WITH PAULINA CHEN

Since the program was developed in 2002, more than 2,000 employment readiness counselors, transition counselors, veterans' counselors, wounded warrior transition counselors and university career counselors have been licensed to teach Ten Steps to a Federal Job® with this guide as the class handout.

The
Resume Place

Catonsville, MD 21228
www.resume-place.com

The Resume Place, Inc.
Federal Career Publishers

P.O. Box 21275, Catonsville, MD 21228
Phone: 888-480-8265
www.resume-place.com
Email: resume@resume-place.com

Printed in the United States of America
Jobseeker's Guide, 7th Ed.
ISBN-13: 978-0-9846671-8-5
ISBN-10: 984667180
Updated May 2015

We have been careful to provide accurate federal job search information in this book, but it is possible that errors and omissions may have been introduced.

Attention Transition Counselors, Veterans' Representatives, Workforce Counselors, Career Counselors: The *Jobseeker's Guide* is a training program "handout" to support the Ten Steps to a Federal Job® workshops and PowerPoint program, which is taught at military bases, universities, one-stops, and DoD agencies worldwide. To be licensed to teach the Ten Steps to a Federal Job® curriculum as a Certified Federal Job Search Trainer® or Certified Federal Career Coach®, go to www.resume-place.com for information on our train-the-trainer program. Since the program was developed in 2002, more than 2,000 have been licensed to teach Ten Steps to a Federal Job® with this guide as the handout.

AUTHOR'S NOTES: Sample resumes are real but fictionalized. All federal applicants have given permission for their resumes to be used as samples for this publication. Privacy policy is strictly enforced.

PUBLICATION TEAM
Cover, Interior Page Design, and Developmental Editing: Paulina Chen
Federal Resume Samples: Bobbi Rossiter (Military Spouse), Natalie Skelton (LinkedIn), Mariano Torres (Veteran), Dan Kim (Networking Job Fair Resume), Blair Richey (Wounded Warrior), Toran Gaal (Wounded Warrior excerpts)
Federal Staffing, Veteran Preference, and Schedule A SME: Charles Clark
Intelligence and DOD Agency Lists: Ellen Lazarus
Updates on Agency List and Chapters: John Gagnon, JD, Ph.D. ABD
Program S Contributor: Bobbi Rossiter
Curriculum Design: Emily Troutman
Wounded Warrior Technical Consulting: Dennis Eley, Jr.
Copyediting: Pamela Sikora
Index: Pilar Wyman

TABLE OF CONTENTS

WHAT'S NEW IN THE 7TH EDITION

TEN STEPS to a FEDERAL JOB®

The most preferred employer for the military after separation and retirement is the U.S. Government. The veterans want a position in public service using their experience and they are familiar with the culture of public service and Defense careers. The spouses want a solid career during their military lifestyle near their military installation. The federal job search and federal resume are highly complex, but this CAN be navigated. The jobseeker needs to learn the Ten Steps to a Federal Job®. This seventh edition is better than ever. Case studies are inspiring and the steps are doable. Follow these steps and you will get Best Qualified, which puts you in the highest category for consideration to be referred, interviewed and selected.

Four new Outline Format Federal Resume samples:

- Dan – separated as 30% or more disabled veteran (CPS) as USMC Rifleman; attended college on GI Bill; got a BS in criminology; wanted a job as FBI Special Agent; landed an internship with IRS while he waits for Special Agent position.

- Mariano – separated as 20% disabled veteran (CP) as USMC Helicopter Crew; attended college on GI Bill; got a BS in Philosophy; couldn't find a job; landed a temporary federal job with the Courts Agency; finally landed a great permanent fed job with DHS.

- Bobbi – U.S. Navy military spouse and Program S registrant seeking career in military transition while husband is following U.S. Navy career.

- Bill – a non-disabled vet (TP) separated from U.S. Army Reserves; complicated Reserves resume with combination of civilian experience. Landed great Contract Specialist career ladder position.

PLUS ...

- NEW information on where to find NAF jobs.

- NEW list of Intelligence agencies.

- NEW Human Resource Staffing and Veterans" Preference, Military Spouse, and Schedule A Reference Section.

- Always great, inspiring information about how to write the Outline Format federal resume with keywords and accomplishments. The HR specialists and hiring managers love this format. It is easy to read and hits the mark to get Best Qualified!

Good luck with your federal job search,
Kathryn Troutman, Author and Publisher, Federal Career
Coach and Ten Steps to a Federal Job® Designer

HOW MANY HATS DO YOU WEAR AT WORK?

Everyone wears different "hats" at work. You can also think about the your skills or leadership in different disciplines or programs. These hats and disciplines are KEYWORDS for your federal resume. Make a list of five to seven hats you wear every day in your job to form the basis of your Outline Format federal resume in Steps 5 and 6 of this guide.

Examples of hats:

- *Supply Analyst*
- *Logistics Manager*
- *Transportation Specialist*
- *Supervisor*
- *Instructor*
- *Team Leader*
- *Database Administrator*
- *Research / Analyst*
- *Contract Officer*
- *Purchasing Specialist*
- *Office Administrator*
- *Advisor*
- *Computer Operations*

Your list of hats:

_____

_____

_____

_____

_____

_____

TEN STEPS TO A FEDERAL JOB®

1. **Review the federal job process.** Start your federal job search with critical federal job information. Find out which agencies, job titles, and grade levels are best suited for you.

2. **Network.** Even with government, who you know is important. This information will remind you that your family, friends, and acquaintances may be a lead to a job in government. Learn strategies to introduce yourself and your job goals.

3. **Research vacancy announcements on USAJOBS.** Learn the fastest way to search for federal jobs on USAJOBS. Search for geographic location and salary first, then drill down to the jobs that sound right for you. You can't write a good federal resume without a target vacancy announcement—even if the announcement is a sample to get you started.

4. **Analyze your core competencies.** In addition to the technical keywords and qualifications, your basic core competencies can stand out as transferrable skills to a new career. Have you been a team leader? Have you analyzed data, resolved conflicts, solved problems and mentored others? These transferable skills and core competencies are popular in new careers! Specialized skills + great interpersonal skills = Best Qualified!

5. **Analyze vacancy announcements for keywords.** Learn how to find keywords in each announcement for your federal resume. Look for the keywords in Duties, Qualifications, Specialized Experience, and KSA lists. Add the keywords into your resume to make it readable, focused, and impressive.

6. **Write your Outline Format and paper federal resumes.** Feature your top skills and accomplishments for each position with keywords. Master the two formats: the Outline Format for online builders, and the paper format for interviews, email attachments, and browser uploads.

7. **KSAs, accomplishments, and questionnaires.** The "rated and ranked" KSAs have been eliminated, but various "how to apply" instructions may still list KSAs that should be covered in the resume. You will also find Assessment Questionnaires with Yes/No and multiple-choice questions.

8. **Apply for jobs with USAJOBS.** Carefully read the "how to apply" instructions, which could be different for each announcement. Get ready to copy and paste your resume into builders, answer questions, write short essays, and fax or upload your documents.

9. **Track and follow up on your applications.** Don't just send in your application and forget about it; you have to manage your federal job search campaign. Learn how to call the personnel office to find out critical information for improving your future applications. Find out how to get your application score.

10. **Interview for a federal job.** Get tips to improve your chances with different types of interviews. Tell your best stories about your accomplishments and leadership skills. Be personable, passionate about the job, and sharp with our list of techniques.

ACCOMPLISHMENT WRITING EXERCISE

Write about a situation, project or problem that you faced in your last or recent position. It is important to make your resume interesting for Human Resources reviewers and managers in order to get referred or selected for an interview!

Describe an accomplishment from your current position or recent volunteer work. Accomplishments are critical for your federal resume, assessment questionnaire essays / examples, and Behavior-Based Interviews.

Write at least three sentences here about your accomplishment:

_____

_____

_____

_____

_____

_____

_____

Write your story with the Resume Place accomplishment tool
www.resume-place.com/ccar_accomplishment

EXAMPLES OF ACCOMPLISHMENTS

Here are federal resume sections demonstrating how to feature both your Duties and your Accomplishments in each job in your resume. Adding accomplishments into two or three of the positions in your Work Experience section will make your resume stand out.

ADMIN PERSONNEL, E-6, United States Navy, Naval Computer and Telecommunications Area Master Station, Hawaii Area Master Computer and Telecommunications Area

- Identified deficiencies in the effectiveness of the file management systems. Independently initiated the restructuring of the correspondence filing system and assisted in the development of a tracking system. As a result there was a drastic improvement to the customer service, productivity and efficiency of the Management Support Department.

First Lieutenant, ADMINISTRATIVE OFFICER-IN-CHARGE, U.S. Army, Combined Joint Task Force, Djibouti, Africa

- Made formal recommendation to command to transition to a new accountability system with more accurate personnel data capture and better personnel data integration with other military systems.
- Spearheaded the development of a more efficient process for submitting Rest & Recuperation requests by leveraging technology resources and transitioning to a completely electronic format. This effort eliminated duplication of data input, increased overall accountability, and streamlined the submission process.

COMMUNICATIONS CHIEF, E-9 /Master Gunnery Sergeant / United States Marine Corps (USMC), I Marine Expeditionary Force, Marine Corps Base Camp, Camp Pendleton, CA

Configured a streamlined process to track and improve asset management for (1,100) items by validating proper employment and forecasting equipment shortages. Studied, introduced, tested, and procured emerging technologies which continued to refine and update the IT infrastructure, reduced cost, and applied measures which decreased waste.

Theater Property Book Asset Visibility Team Chief, G4 United States Army Forces, Central Command Camp Arifjan, Kuwait

PROPERTY MANAGEMENT: Managed 13.5 million items of equipment valued at $73 billion and oversaw property policies and procedures in the United States Central Command area, including inter-service agreements. Recognized as the theater subject matter expert on equipment transactions and frequently consulted by others.

- Coordinated with the Theater Deployment/Redeployment Operations cell to improve the unit pre-deployment site survey by quickly addressing Property Book Officer issues to over 80 Property Book Officers and provided oversight for over 3,000 units.

STEP 1

Review the Federal Job Process

YOUR FEDERAL JOB SEARCH GOALS | STEP 1

TARGET AGENCIES

What are your target agencies?

TARGET JOB TITLES AND SERIES

What is your current military job title?

How many years of specialized experience do you have?

Which federal job titles or series seem correct for you?

GRADE AND SALARY

What is your current military rank?

What is your current military salary?

What will be your target federal grade level?

What will your salary be, if you apply to a pay band agency?

CROSSWALK FROM MOC TO GS

This website is the first and only Military Occupational Code (MOC) to GS crosswalk and is sponsored by the State of Maryland. Match your MOC to GS interests online in just minutes!

Go to the Military to Federal Jobs Crosswalk: **www.mil2fedjobs.com**

A

AbilityOne Commission
Access Board
Administration for Children and Families
Administration on Aging (AOA)
Administration for Community Living
Administration for Native Americans
Administration on Developmental Disabilities
Administrative Conference of the United States
Administrative Office of the U.S. Courts
Advisory Council on Historic Preservation
African Development Foundation
Agency for Healthcare Research and Quality
Agency for International Development
Agency for Toxic Substances and Disease Registry
Agricultural Marketing Service
Agricultural Research Service
Agriculture Department
Air Force
Air Force Reserve
Alcohol and Tobacco Tax and Trade Bureau
American Battle Monuments Commission
AmeriCorps
AMTRAK (National Railroad Passenger Corporation)
Animal and Plant Health Inspection Service
Appalachian Regional Commission
Architect of the Capitol
Arctic Research Commission
Armed Forces Retirement Home
Arms Control and International Security, Under
    Secretary for
Army
Army Corps of Engineers (USACE)
Arthritis and Musculoskeletal Interagency
    Coordinating Committee

B

Botanic Garden (USBG)
Broadcasting Board of Governors (BBG) (Voice of
    America, Radio/TV Marti, and more)
Bureau of Alcohol, Tobacco, Firearms, and
    Explosives (ATF)
Bureau of Economic Analysis
Bureau of Engraving and Printing
Bureau of Indian Affairs

Bureau of Industry and Security
Bureau of International Labor Affairs
Bureau of Labor Statistics
Bureau of Land Management
Bureau of Prisons
Bureau of Public Debt
Bureau of Reclamation
Bureau of Safety and Environmental Enforcement
Bureau of the Fiscal Service
Bureau of Transportation Statistics

C

Capitol Police
Census Bureau
Center for Nutrition Policy and Promotion
Centers for Disease Control and Prevention (CDC)
Centers for Medicare & Medicaid Services
Central Intelligence Agency (CIA)
Chemical Safety and Hazard Investigation Board
Citizenship and Immigration Services (USCIS)
Civilian Radioactive Waste Management
Coast Guard (USCG)
Commerce Department
Commission of Fine Arts
Commission on Civil Rights
Commission on International Religious Freedom
Committee for the Implementation of Textile
    Agreements
Community Oriented Policing Services
Community Planning and Development
Compliance, Office of
Comptroller of the Currency, Office of the
Congressional Budget Office
Congressional Research Service
Consular Affairs Bureau
Consumer Financial Protection Bureau

Consumer Product Safety Commission (CPSC)
Cooperative State Research, Education, and
    Extension Service
Copyright Office
Corporation for National and Community Service
Corps of Engineers
Council of Economic Advisers
Council on Environmental Quality
Court of Appeals for the Armed Forces
Court of Appeals for the Federal Circuit
Court of Appeals for Veterans Claims
Court of Federal Claims
Court of International Trade
Court Services and Offender Supervision Agency for
    the District of Columbia
Customs and Border Protection

D

Defense Acquisition University
Defense Advanced Research Projects Agency
Defense Commissary Agency
Defense Contract Audit Agency
Defense Contract Management Agency
Defense Finance and Accounting Service
Defense Information Systems Agency
Defense Intelligence Agency (DIA)
Defense Legal Services Agency
Defense Logistics Agency
Defense Nuclear Facilities Safety Board
Defense Security Cooperation Agency
Defense Security Service
Defense Threat Reduction Agency
Delaware River Basin Commission
Denali Commission
Department of Agriculture (USDA)
Department of Commerce (DOC)
Department of Defense (DOD)
Department of Education (ED)
Department of Energy (DOE)
Department of Health and Human Services (HHS)
Department of Homeland Security (DHS)
Department of Housing and Urban Development
    (HUD)
Department of the Interior (DOI)
Department of Justice (DOJ)
Department of Labor (DOL)
Department of State (DOS)
Department of Transportation (DOT)
Department of the Treasury

Department of Veterans Affairs (VA)
Director of National Intelligence, Office of
Disability Employment Policy, Office of
Domestic Policy Council
Drug Enforcement Administration (DEA)

E

Economic Adjustment Office
Economic Analysis Bureau
Economic and Statistics Administration
Economic, Business and Agricultural Affairs
Economic Development Administration
Economic Research Service
Election Assistance Commission
Elementary and Secondary Education, Office of
Employee Benefits Security Administration
Employment and Training Administration
Employment Standards Administration
Endangered Species Program
Energy Efficiency and Renewable Energy
Energy Information Administration
English Language Acquisition Office
Environmental Management
Environmental Protection Agency (EPA)
Equal Employment Opportunity Commission (EEOC)
Executive Office for Immigration Review
Export-Import Bank of the United States

F

Fair Housing and Equal Opportunity, Office of
Faith-Based and Community Initiatives Office
Farm Credit System Insurance Corporation
Farm Service Agency (FSA)
Federal Accounting Standards Advisory Board
Federal Aviation Administration
Federal Bureau of Investigation (FBI)
Federal Bureau of Prisons
Federal Communications Commission (FCC)
Federal Deposit Insurance Corporation (FDIC)
Federal Election Commission (FEC)
Federal Emergency Management Agency (FEMA)
Federal Financing Bank
Federal Highway Administration
Federal Home Loan Mortgage Corporation
Federal Housing Administration
Federal Housing Enterprise Oversight
Federal Housing Finance Board
Federal Judicial Center
Federal Labor Relations Authority

Federal Law Enforcement Training Center
Federal Maritime Commission
Federal Mediation and Conciliation Service
Federal Mine Safety and Health Review Commission
Federal Motor Carrier Safety Administration
Federal National Mortgage Association
Federal Protective Service
Federal Railroad Administration
Federal Reserve System
Federal Retirement Thrift Investment Board
Federal Trade Commission (FTC)
Federal Transit Administration
Financial Management Service
Fiscal Responsibility and Reform Commission
Fiscal Service Bureau
Fish and Wildlife Service
Food and Drug Administration (FDA)
Food and Nutrition Service
Food Safety and Inspection Service
Foreign Agricultural Service
Forest Service
Fossil Energy

G

General Services Administration
Geological Survey (USGS)
Global Affairs
Government Accountability Office (GAO)
Government Ethics, Office of
Government National Mortgage Association
Government Publishing Office
Grain Inspection, Packers, and Stockyards
    Administration

H

Health Resources and Services Administration
Healthy Homes and Lead Hazard Control Office
Helsinki Commission
Holocaust Memorial Museum
House of Representatives
House Office of Inspector General
House Office of the Clerk

I

Immigration and Customs Enforcement
Indian Arts and Crafts Board
Indian Health Service
Industrial College of the Armed Forces
Information Resource Management College

Institute of Education Sciences
Institute of Museum and Library Services
Institute of Peace
Inter-American Foundation
Interior Department
Internal Revenue Service (IRS)
International Broadcasting Bureau (IBB)
International Trade Administration (ITA)

J

Job Corps
Joint Chiefs of Staff
Joint Forces Staff College
Joint Military Intelligence College
Joint Program Executive Office for Chemical and
    Biological Defense
Judicial Circuit Courts of Appeal
Judicial Panel on Multidistrict Litigation
Justice Programs, Office of
Juvenile Justice and Delinquency Prevention,
    Office of

L

Labor Department
Labor Statistics, Bureau of
Land Management, Bureau of
Legal Services Corporation
Library of Congress

M

Marine Mammal Commission
Marine Corps
Maritime Administration
Marketing and Regulatory Programs
Marshals Service
Mediation and Conciliation Service
Medicaid
Medicare Payment Advisory Commission
Merit Systems Protection Board
Migratory Bird Conservation Commission
Military Postal Service Agency
Mine Safety and Health Administration
Minority Business Development Agency
Mint
Missile Defense Agency
Mississippi River Commission
Multifamily Housing Office

N

National Aeronautics and Space Administration (NASA)
National Agricultural Statistics Service
National AIDS Policy Office
National Archives and Records Administration (NARA)
National Capital Planning Commission
National Cemetery Administration
National Council on Disability
National Counterintelligence Executive, Office of
National Credit Union Administration
National Defense University
National Drug Intelligence Center
National Endowment for the Arts
National Endowment for the Humanities
National Flood Insurance Program
National Gallery of Art
National Geospatial-Intelligence Agency
National Guard Bureau
National Highway Traffic Safety Administration
National Indian Gaming Commission
National Institute of Corrections
National Institute of Justice
National Institute of Mental Health
National Institute of Occupational Safety and Health
National Institute of Standards and Technology (NIST)
National Institutes of Health (NIH)
National Labor Relations Board
National Laboratories
National Marine Fisheries
National Mediation Board
National Nuclear Security Administration
National Ocean Service
National Oceanic and Atmospheric Administration (NOAA)
National Park Service
National Science Foundation
National Security Agency
National Security Council
National Technical Information Service
National Telecommunications and Information Administration
National Transportation Safety Board (NTSB)
National War College
National Weather Service
Natural Resources Conservation Service
Navy, Department of the

Nuclear Energy, Science and Technology
Nuclear Regulatory Commission
Nuclear Waste Technical Review Board

O

Occupational Safety & Health Administration (OSHA)
Ocean Energy Management Bureau
Office of Government Ethics
Office of Management and Budget (OMB)
Office of National Drug Control Policy (ONDCP)
Office of Personnel Management
Office of Science and Technology Policy
Office of Special Counsel
Office of Thrift Supervision
Overseas Private Investment Corporation

P

Pacific Northwest Electric Power and Conservation Planning Council
Pardon Attorney Office
Parole Commission
Patent and Trademark Office
Peace Corps
Pension Benefit Guaranty Corporation
Pentagon Force Protection Agency
Pipeline and Hazardous Materials Safety Commission
Policy Development and Research
Political Affairs
Postal Regulatory Commission
Postal Service (USPS)
Postsecondary Education, Office of
Power Administrations
Presidio Trust
Public Diplomacy and Public Affairs
Public and Indian Housing

R

Radio and TV Marti (Español)
Radio Free Asia (RFA)
Radio Free Europe/Radio Liberty (RFE/RL)
Railroad Retirement Board
Reclamation Bureau
Regulatory Information Service Center
Rehabilitation Services Administration
Research and Innovative Technology Administration
Research, Education, and Economics
Risk Management Agency
Rural Business and Cooperative Programs

Rural Development
Rural Housing Service
Rural Utilities Service

S

Safety and Environmental Enforcement Bureau
Saint Lawrence Seaway Development Corporation
Science and Technology Policy Office
Scientific and Technical Information Office
Secret Service
Securities and Exchange Commission (SEC)
Selective Service System
Senate
Small Business Administration (SBA)
Smithsonian Institution
Social Security Administration (SSA)
Social Security Advisory Board
Southeastern Power Administration
Special Education and Rehabilitative Services
State Department
Stennis Center for Public Service
Student Financial Assistance Programs
Substance Abuse and Mental Health Services
     Administration
Supreme Court of the United States
Surface Mining, Reclamation, and Enforcement
Surface Transportation Board
Susquehanna River Basin Commission

T

Tax Court
Taxpayer Advocacy Panel
Taxpayer Advocacy Service
Tennessee Valley Authority
Trade and Development Agency
Transportation Security Administration
Treasury Department
TRICARE Management
Trustee Program

U

U.S. International Trade Commission
U.S. Mission to the United Nations
U.S. National Central Bureau – Interpol
U.S. Trade Representative
Unified Combatant Commands
Uniformed Services University of the Health
     Sciences

V

Veterans Benefits Administration
Veterans Employment and Training Service
Veterans Health Administration
Vietnam Education Foundation
Voice of America (VOA)

W

Weather Service
West Point
Western Area Power Administration
White House
White House Office of Administration
Women's Bureau
Woodrow Wilson International Center for Scholars

DEPARTMENT OF DEFENSE EMPLOYMENT OPPORTUNITIES

The Department of Defense (DOD) is an Executive Department in the U.S. Government. DOD employs over three million military and civilians in three military departments (Army, Navy, and Air Force), the National Guard and various Reserves services, and a number of subordinate agencies. This chart provides information about many of the agencies that employ civilians. After accessing the website, you can find information about employment either by clicking on "careers" or by entering the term "careers" or "employment" in the search bar.

Agency (Acronym)	Approx. # of Staff	Website	Types of Positions
Department of Army	300,000+ civilians	http://www.army.mil Civilian Personnel Sites: http://cpol.army.mil and http://www.armycivilianservice.com	Information technology; communications; audit and finance; security and law enforcement; engineering and science; legal; contracting; logistics and operations management; medical; public affairs; transportation; electrical installation and maintenance; warehousing and stock handling; inventory management; intelligence; international affairs; program managers
Department of Navy	200,000+ civilians	http://www.navy.mil Civilian Personnel Site: http://www.donhr.navy.mil	Information technology; communications; audit and finance; security and law enforcement; engineering and science; legal; contracting; logistics and operations management; medical; public affairs; transportation; electrical installation and maintenance; warehousing and stock handling; inventory management; intelligence; international affairs; program managers
Department of the Air Force	180,000 civilians	http://www.af.mil Civilian Careers: http://www.afciviliancareers.com/	Information technology; communications; audit and finance; security and law enforcement; engineering and science; legal; contracting; logistics and operations management; medical; public affairs; transportation; electrical installation and maintenance; warehousing and stock handling; inventory management; intelligence; international affairs; program managers
Defense Advanced Research Projects Agency (DARPA)	200+	http://www.darpa.mil	Engineering research; adaptive technologies; information innovation; microelectromechanical systems (MEMS), electronics, computing, photonics and biotechnology; strategic technology; tactical technology
Defense Commissary Agency (DeCA)	15,000+	http://www.commissaries.com	Operates more than 250 commissaries worldwide — store workers and clerks; supply technicians, managers; customer service representatives

Agency (Acronym)	Approx. # of Staff	Website	Types of Positions
Defense Contract Audit Agency (DCAA)	5,000+	http://www.dcaa.mil	Finance; auditors; CPAs
Defense Contract Management Agency (DCMA)	10,000+ civilians; 20,000 contractors	http://www.dcma.mil	Contract specialists; contract price analysts; auditors; supply and procurement; acquisition support; property management; software acquisition management; transportation; safety; quality assurance
Defense Finance and Accounting Service (DFAS)	12,000+	http://www.dfas.mil	Accountants; auditors; financial managers; information technology specialists; contract specialists
Defense Information Systems Agency (DISA)	6,000+	http://www.disa.mil	Contract specialists; communications services; information technology specialists; acquisition support; computer scientists; program analysts; operations research analysts; purchasing agents
Defense Intelligence Agency (DIA)	16,500 civilian and military	http://www.dia.mil	Intelligence collection and analysis; radar, acoustic, nuclear, chemical and biological intelligence; information management and information technology; foreign language specialists; program analysts
Defense Logistics Agency (DLA)	27,000 civilian and military	http://www.dla.mil	Supply managers; property disposal specialists; logistics specialists; contract specialists; engineers; information technology specialists, product specialists (quality assurance/ technical)
Defense Security Cooperation Agency (DSCA)	750+ security personnel in regional centers and working with international students	http://dsca.mil	Foreign military sales; strategic planning & integration; information technology; public health advisors; contracting specialists; program analysts; security assistance analysts; financial management analysts; humanitarian assistance program coordinators; FMS analysts
Defense Security Service (DSS)	N/A	http://www.dss.mil/	Counterintelligence; foreign ownership, control or influence (FOCI) professionals; information system security; industrial security; information technology; security education and training (instructor/visual information specialists)
Defense Technical Information Center (DTIC)	N/A	http://www.dtic.mil	Information technology, network security, and database managers; customer service personnel; librarians; technical information specialists; graphic designers; project managers; program and management analysts; web developers; digital preservation specialists; technical writers/editors; marketing specialists; reference and research personnel; trainers

DEPARTMENT OF DEFENSE EMPLOYMENT OPPORTUNITIES CONT.

Agency (Acronym)	Approx. # of Staff	Website	Types of Positions
Defense Threat Reduction Agency (DTRA)	2,000	http://www.dtra.mil	Subject Matter Experts on weapons of mass destruction (WMD); physical scientists; engineers; mathematicians; forensics; technology specialists
DOD Education Activity (DODEA)	12,500+ (in 191 schools worldwide)	http://www.dodea.edu	Teachers; instructional specialists; educational aids; school nurses; speech pathologists; school occupational therapists; librarians and library technicians
Missile Defense Agency (MDA)	8,500+	http://www.mda.mil	Engineers; scientists; mathematicians; researchers; computer professionals; information technology specialists; communications specialists; program managers; procurement analysts; contracts management; logistics managers; operations research specialists
National Geospatial-Intelligence Agency (NGA)	14,500+ civilians, military and contractors	https://www1.nga.mil/Careers/Pages/default.aspx	Geospatial intelligence (GEOINT) analysts; imagery scientists; information assurance specialists; project scientists; software, web, and systems engineers; visualization specialists; contract analysts; program managers; counterintelligence officers
National Reconnaissance Office (NRO)	3,000+	http://www.nro.gov	Scientists; engineers; communications specialists; acquisition managers (workforce consists of personnel from DOD, CIA, NGA, NSA, and U.S. Air Force)
Office of Inspector General (DODIG)	1,400	http://www.dodig.mil	Auditors; investigators; special agents; analysts
U.S. Army Corps of Engineers (USACE)	37,000 civilians	http://www.usace.army.mil	Accountants and financial analysts; attorneys; civil works specialists; construction control representatives; contract specialists; engineers; emergency operations specialists; construction managers; disaster response specialists; environmental specialists; logistics specialists; natural resources specialists; park rangers; project managers; real estate managers; research & development personnel; resource management specialists; strategic planners and analysts; trades (e.g., electrician, welding, lock & dam operator, etc.)
Pentagon Force Protection Agency (PFPA)	N/A	http://www.pfpa.mil/	Law enforcement officers (Pentagon Police); criminal investigative and protective agents; threat management agents and technicians; physical security personnel; information technology specialists

Agency (Acronym)	Approx. # of Staff	Website	Types of Positions
Defense Health Agency (DHA)	N/A	http://tricare.mil/tma/default.aspx	Contract and acquisition managers; nurse specialists; physicians; pharmacists; medical technologists; health care scientists; service representatives; conflict resolution professionals; graphic designers; records management; program evaluation and analysis; data management
Washington Headquarters Services	1,200 civilian and military; 2,000 contract employees	http://www.whs.mil	Essential administrative and management services in support of DOD operations including: contracting and procurement; acquisition services; supplies and equipment services; information management; records management; graphics services; budget, financial reporting and analysis; information technology; IT training; risk mitigation; security assessments; telecommunications; safety; environmental management; occupational safety and health; personnel security

INTELLIGENCE COMMUNITY EMPLOYMENT OPPORTUNITIES

In 2004, the Office of the Director of National Intelligence (ODNI) was established to manage the efforts of the Intelligence Community (IC). The work of 17 civilian and military services IC agencies, branches, offices, and bureaus is now consolidated under the ODNI. Each of the organizations within the IC operates under its own directive. This chart provides information about many of the agencies that employ civilians. After accessing the website, you can find information about employment either by clicking on "careers" or entering the term "careers" or "employment" in the search bar.

The Office of Personnel Management's (OPM) Intelligence Series is GS-0132. IC entities typically do not publicly disclose their budget or number of employees.

Information about careers throughout the IC can be found either via USAJOBS (for some but not all of the IC organizations) or at individual entity websites listed below. The website www.intelligence.gov brings together information on career opportunities among the 17 IC agencies across the U.S. and overseas. It is an excellent resource for exploring career choices and applying for positions. Some intelligence agencies offer internships and scholarship opportunities.

Agency (Acronym)	Website	Description / Mission
Office of the Director of National Intelligence	www.odni.gov Careers: http://www.odni.gov/index.php/careers/careers-at-odni	The Director of National Intelligence (DNI) heads up the ODNI and serves as the principal advisor to the President, the National Security Council, and the Homeland Security Council. The ODNI's focus is to promote a more integrated and collaborative IC.
Central Intelligence Agency (CIA)	www.cia.gov Careers: https://www.cia.gov/careers/opportunities	The CIA is separated into four basic components: the National Clandestine Service, the Directorate of Intelligence, the Directorate of Science & Technology, and the Directorate of Support.
Defense Intelligence Agency	www.dia.mil Careers: www.dia.mil/careers.aspx	Department of Defense combat support agency. With more than 16,500 military and civilian employees worldwide, DIA is a major producer and manager of foreign military intelligence and provides military intelligence in support of U.S. military planning and operations and weapon systems acquisition.
Federal Bureau of Investigation (FBI) National Security Branch	www.fbi.gov Careers: https://www.fbijobs.gov/index.asp	Established to combine the missions, capabilities, and resources of the FBI's counterterrorism, counterintelligence, and intelligence elements. The NSB also includes the Terrorist Screening Center, which provides crucial, actionable intelligence to state and local law enforcement, and the High-Value Detainee Interrogation Group, which collects intelligence from key terror suspects to prevent attacks against the U.S. and its allies.

Agency (Acronym)	Website	Description / Mission
National Geospatial-Intelligence Agency (NGA)	www.nga.mil Careers: https://www1.nga.mil/Careers/Pages/default.aspx	Provides timely, relevant, and accurate geospatial intelligence in support of national security objectives. NGA provides support to civilian and military leaders and contributes to the state of readiness of U.S. military forces. NGA also contributes to humanitarian efforts such as tracking floods and fires, and to peacekeeping.
National Reconnaissance Office (NRO)	www.nro.gov Careers: www.nro.gov/careers/careers.html	The NRO's workforce consists of personnel from the DOD, Central Intelligence Agency (CIA), National Geospatial-Intelligence Agency (NGA), and National Security Agency (NSA). The Air Force and CIA comprise the majority of the military and civilian population. Designs, builds, and operates the nation's reconnaissance satellites to warn of potential trouble spots around the world, help plan military operations, and monitor the environment.
National Security Agency/Central Security Service	www.nsa.gov Careers: www.nsa.gov/careers	At the forefront of communications and information technology, the nation's cryptologic organization coordinates, directs, and performs highly specialized activities to protect U.S. information systems and to produce foreign signals intelligence information. NSA is also one of the most important centers of foreign language analysis and is said to be the largest employer of mathematicians in the United States and perhaps the world. Its workforce represents an unusual combination of specialties: analysts, engineers, physicists, mathematicians, linguists, computer scientists, researchers, as well as customer relations specialists, security officers, data flow experts, managers, administrative officers, and clerical assistants.
Drug Enforcement Administration (DEA) Office of National Security Intelligence	www.dea.gov Careers: www.dea.gov/careers/occupations.shtml	Enforces the controlled substance laws and regulations of the United States. DEA's Office of National Security Intelligence (ONSI) became a member of the IC in 2006. ONSI facilitates full and appropriate intelligence coordination and information sharing with other members of the U.S. Intelligence Community and homeland security elements. Its goal is to enhance the U.S.'s efforts to reduce the supply of drugs, protect national security, and combat global terrorism.
Department of Energy Office of Intelligence & Counter-Intelligence	www.energy.gov Careers: www.energy.gov/jobs/jobs	Intelligence and counterintelligence activities throughout the DOE complex, including nearly 30 intelligence and counterintelligence offices nationwide.
Department of Homeland Security (DHS) Office of Intelligence & Analysis	www.dhs.gov Careers: www.dhs.gov/careers	Uses information and intelligence from multiple sources to identify and assess current and future threats to the U.S. DHS Intelligence focuses on four strategic areas: promote understanding of threats through intelligence analysis; collect information and intelligence pertinent to homeland security; share information necessary for action; and manage intelligence for the homeland security enterprise.

Agency (Acronym)	Website	Description / Mission
State Department Bureau of Intelligence & Research	www.state.gov Careers: www.state.gov/careers	Provides timely, objective analysis of global developments as well as real-time insights from all-source intelligence. It serves as the focal point within the Department of State for all policy issues and activities involving the Intelligence Community. INR's expert, independent foreign affairs analysts draw on all-source intelligence, diplomatic reporting, INR's public opinion polling, and interaction with U.S. and foreign scholars.
Coast Guard Intelligence	www.uscg.mil Careers: www.uscg.mil/civilian	The Coast Guard's persistent presence in the maritime domain, due to its diverse mission sets and broad legal authorities, allows it to fill a unique niche within the Intelligence Community. Coast Guard Intelligence strives to create decision advantage to advance U.S. interests by providing timely, actionable, and relevant intelligence to shape Coast Guard operations, planning, and decision-making, and to support national and homeland security intelligence requirements.
Air Force Intelligence, Surveillance, & Reconnaissance (AF ISR)	www.af.mil Careers: www.afciviliancareers.com/	The Air Force ISR Agency organizes, trains, equips, and presents forces to conduct intelligence, surveillance, and reconnaissance for combatant commanders and the nation. The AF ISR Agency commander serves as the Service Cryptologic Element under NSA, and oversees Air Force Signals Intelligence activities. The AF ISR Agency has more than 19,000 military and civilian members serving at 72 locations worldwide and commands several subcomponents.
Army Intelligence and Security Command (G-2)	www.army.mil Careers: www.cpol.army.mil	Coordinates the five major military intelligence (MI) disciplines within the Army: Imagery Intelligence, Signals Intelligence, Human Intelligence, Measurement and Signature Intelligence, and Counterintelligence and Security Countermeasures.
U.S. Marine Corps Intelligence Activity	www.hqmc.marines.mil/intelligence Careers: www.hqmc.marines.mil/intelligence/CivilianCareer.aspx	Produces tactical and operational intelligence for battlefield support. Staff expertise includes: geospatial intelligence, advanced geospatial intelligence, signals intelligence, human intelligence, counterintelligence; and ensures there is a single synchronized strategy for the development of the Marine Corps Intelligence, Surveillance, and Reconnaissance Enterprise.
U.S. Navy, Office of Naval Intelligence (ONI)	www.oni.navy.mil Careers: www.oni.navy.mil/Join_US/Civilian_Careers/Civilian_Careers.html	ONI employs more than 3,000 military, civilian, mobilized reservists, and contractor personnel worldwide, including analysts, scientists, engineers, specialists, and technicians. While ONI is the largest Naval Intelligence organization with the largest concentration of Naval Intelligence civilians, most of Naval Intelligence comprises active duty military personnel, serving throughout the world.

NON-APPROPRIATED FUND (NAF) JOBS | STEP 1

NAF jobs are federal jobs located on military bases worldwide, but they are different from federal civil service employment, because the monies used to pay the salaries of NAF employees come from a different source. Civil service positions are paid for by money appropriated by Congress. NAF employee are paid from nonappropriated funds of Army and Air Force Exchange Service, Navy Exchange Service Command, Marine Corps exchanges, or any other armed forces organization for the comfort, pleasure, contentment, or physical or mental improvement of members of the armed forces. Benefits are great!

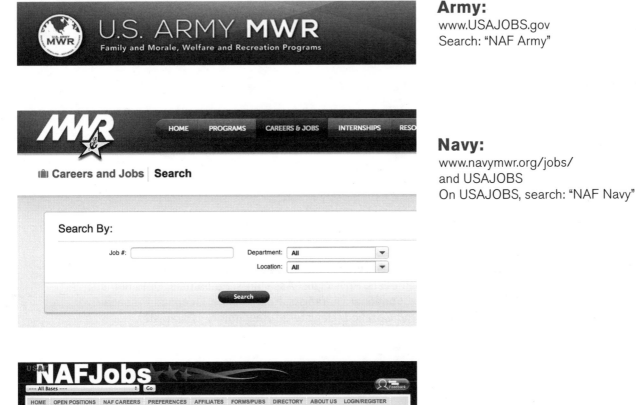

Army:
www.USAJOBS.gov
Search: "NAF Army"

Navy:
www.navymwr.org/jobs/
and USAJOBS
On USAJOBS, search: "NAF Navy"

Air Force:
www.nafjobs.org/viewjobs.aspx
On USAJOBS, search "NAF Air Force"

Marine Corps:
www.usmc-mccs.org/careers/ (click on Prospective Employees under Job Search & Apply)
On USAJOBS, search "NAF USMC"

 **MCCS Civilian Careers**
Marine Corps Community Services | *Serving Those Who Serve*

EXCEPTED SERVICE AGENCIES

These are some of the major excepted service agencies. All their vacancies may or may not be posted on USAJOBS, so you should view their agency website for additional employment opportunities.

- Federal Reserve System, Board of Governors
- Central Intelligence Agency
- Defense Intelligence Agency
- U.S. Department of State
- Federal Bureau of Investigation
- General Accounting Office
- Agency for International Development
- National Security Agency
- U.S. Nuclear Regulatory Commission
- Postal Rates Commission
- Postal Service
- Tennessee Valley Authority
- U.S. AID
- United States Mission to the United Nations

Department of Veterans Affairs, Health Services and Research Administration:
Physicians, Dentists, Nurses, Nurse Anesthetists, Physicians' Assistants, Podiatrists, Optometrists, Expanded-function Dental Auxiliaries, Occupational Therapists, Pharmacists, Licensed Practical/ Vocational Nurses, Physical Therapists, and Certified/Registered Respiratory Therapists.

Judicial Branch

Legislative Branch

Public International Organizations:
- International Monetary Fund
- Pan American Health Organization
- United Nations Children's Fund
- United Nations Development Program
- United Nations Institute
- United Nations Population Fund
- United Nations Secretariat
- World Bank, International Finance Corporation (IFC), and the Multilateral Investment Guarantee Agency (MIGA)

Find a link to the list of Excepted Service Agencies and Excepted Service Positions at:
www.resume-place.com/resources/useful-links/

OCCUPATIONAL GROUPS AND SERIES |

Here is an excerpt of job titles from the HANDBOOK OF OCCUPATIONAL GROUPS AND FAMILIES, U.S. Office of Personnel Management Office of Classification, Washington, DC. See the full listing at: www.opm.gov/policy-data-oversight/classification-qualifications/classifying-general-schedule-positions/occupationalhandbook.pdf

Carefully reading the qualifications requirements for various occupational series at the different grades will help you make realistic decisions about what jobs to pursue (title, series, and grade) and may save you from wasting time applying for jobs where you simply don't meet those requirements.

GS-000 – MISCELLANEOUS OCCUPATIONS GROUP (NOT ELSEWHERE CLASSIFIED)

This group includes all classes of positions the duties of which are to administer, supervise, or perform work, which cannot be included in other occupational groups either because the duties are unique, or because they are complex and come in part under various groups.

Series in this group are:
GS-006 - Correctional Institution Administration Series
GS-007 - Correctional Officer Series
GS-011 - Bond Sales Promotion Series
GS-018 - Safety and Occupational Health Management Series
GS-019 - Safety Technician Series
GS-020 - Community Planning Series
GS-021 - Community Planning Technician Series
GS-023 - Outdoor Recreation Planning Series
GS-025 - Park Ranger Series
GS-028 - Environmental Protection Specialist Series
GS-029 - Environmental Protection Assistant Series
GS-030 - Sports Specialist Series
GS-050 - Funeral Directing Series
GS-060 - Chaplain Series
GS-062 - Clothing Design Series
GS-072 - Fingerprint Identification Series
GS-080 - Security Administration Series
GS-081 - Fire Protection and Prevention Series
GS-082 - United States Marshal Series
GS-083 - Police Series
GS-084 - Nuclear Materials Courier Series
GS-085 - Security Guard Series
GS-086 - Security Clerical and Assistance Series
GS-090 - Guide Series
GS-095 - Foreign Law Specialist Series
GS-099 - General Student Trainee Series

GS-100 – SOCIAL SCIENCE, PSYCHOLOGY, AND WELFARE GROUP

This group includes all classes of positions the duties of which are to advise on, administer, supervise, or perform research or other professional and scientific work, subordinate technical work, or related clerical work in one or more of the social sciences; in psychology; in social work; in recreational activities; or in the administration of public welfare and insurance programs.

Series in this group are:
GS-101 - Social Science Series
GS-102 - Social Science Aid and Technician Series
GS-105 - Social Insurance Administration Series
GS-106 - Unemployment Insurance Series
GS-107 - Health Insurance Administration Series
GS-110 - Economist Series
GS-119 - Economics Assistant Series
GS-130 - Foreign Affairs Series
GS-131 - International Relations Series
GS-132 - Intelligence Series
GS-134 - Intelligence Aid and Clerk Series
GS-135 - Foreign Agricultural Affairs Series
GS-136 - International Cooperation Series
GS-140 - Manpower Research and Analysis Series
GS-142 - Manpower Development Series
GS-150 - Geography Series
GS-160 - Civil Rights Analysis Series
GS-170 - History Series
GS-180 - Psychology Series
GS-181 - Psychology Aid and Technician Series
GS-184 - Sociology Series
GS-185 - Social Work Series
GS-186 - Social Services Aid and Assistant Series
GS-187 - Social Services Series
GS-188 - Recreation Specialist Series
GS-189 - Recreation Aid and Assistant Series
GS-190 - General Anthropology Series
GS-193 - Archeology Series
GS-199 - Social Science Student Trainee Series

GS-200 – HUMAN RESOURCES MANAGEMENT GROUP

This group includes all classes of positions the duties of which are to advise on, administer, supervise, or perform work involved in the various phases of human resources management.

Series in this group are:
GS-201 - Human Resources Management Series
GS-203 - Human Resources Assistance Series
GS-241 - Mediation Series
GS-243 - Apprenticeship and Training Series
GS-244 - Labor Management Relations Examining Series
GS-260 - Equal Employment Opportunity Series
GS-299 - Human Resources Management Student Trainee Series

GS-300 – GENERAL ADMINISTRATIVE, CLERICAL, AND OFFICE SERVICES GROUP

This group includes all classes of positions the duties of which are to administer, supervise, or perform work involved in management analysis; stenography, typing, correspondence, and secretarial work; mail and file work; the operation of office appliances; the operation of communications equipment, use of codes and ciphers, and procurement of the most effective and efficient communications services; the operation of microform equipment, peripheral equipment, mail processing equipment, duplicating equipment, and copier/duplicating equipment; and other work of a general clerical and administrative nature.

Series in this group are:
GS-301 - Miscellaneous Administration and Program Series
GS-302 - Messenger Series
GS-303 - Miscellaneous Clerk and Assistant Series
GS-304 - Information Receptionist Series
GS-305 - Mail and File Series
GS-309 - Correspondence Clerk Series
GS-312 - Clerk-Stenographer and Reporter Series
GS-313 - Work Unit Supervising Series
GS-318 - Secretary Series
GS-319 - Closed Microphone Reporting Series
GS-322 - Clerk-Typist Series
GS-326 - Office Automation Clerical and Assistance Series
GS-332 - Computer Operation Series
GS-335 - Computer Clerk and Assistant Series

GS-340 - Program Management Series
GS-341 - Administrative Officer Series
GS-342 - Support Services Administration Series
GS-343 - Management and Program Analysis Series
GS-344 - Management and Program Clerical and Assistance Series
GS-346 - Logistics Management Series
GS-350 - Equipment Operator Series
GS-356 - Data Transcriber Series
GS-357 - Coding Series
GS-360 - Equal Opportunity Compliance Series
GS-361 - Equal Opportunity Assistance Series
GS-382 - Telephone Operating Series
GS-390 - Telecommunications Processing Series
GS-391 - Telecommunications Series
GS-392 - General Telecommunications Series
GS-394 - Communications Clerical Series
GS-399 - Administration and Office Support Student Trainee Series

GS-400 – NATURAL RESOURCES MANAGEMENT AND BIOLOGICAL SCIENCES GROUP

This group includes all classes of positions the duties of which are to advise on, administer, supervise, or perform research or other professional and scientific work or subordinate technical work in any of the fields of science concerned with living organisms, their distribution, characteristics, life processes, and adaptations and relations to the environment; the soil, its properties and distribution, and the living organisms growing in or on the soil, and the management, conservation, or utilization thereof for particular purposes or uses.

Series in this group are:
GS-401 - General Natural Resources Management and Biological Sciences Series
GS-403 - Microbiology Series
GS-404 - Biological Science Technician Series
GS-405 - Pharmacology Series
GS-408 - Ecology Series
GS-410 - Zoology Series
GS-413 - Physiology Series
GS-414 - Entomology Series
GS-415 - Toxicology Series
GS-421 - Plant Protection Technician Series
GS-430 - Botany Series
GS-434 - Plant Pathology Series
GS-435 - Plant Physiology Series
GS-437 - Horticulture Series

GS-440 - Genetics Series
GS-454 - Rangeland Management Series
GS-455 - Range Technician Series
GS-457 - Soil Conservation Series
GS-458 - Soil Conservation Technician Series
GS-459 - Irrigation System Operation Series
GS-460 - Forestry Series
GS-462 - Forestry Technician Series
GS-470 - Soil Science Series
GS-471 - Agronomy Series
GS-480 - Fish and Wildlife Administration Series
GS-482 - Fish Biology Series
GS-485 - Wildlife Refuge Management Series
GS-486 - Wildlife Biology Series
GS-487 - Animal Science Series
GS-499 - Biological Science Student Trainee Series

GS-500 – ACCOUNTING AND BUDGET GROUP

This group includes all classes of positions the duties of which are to advise on, administer, supervise, or perform professional, technical, or related clerical work of an accounting, budget administration, related financial management or similar nature.

Series in this group are:
GS-501 - Financial Administration and Program Series
GS-503 - Financial Clerical and Technician Series
GS-505 - Financial Management Series
GS-510 - Accounting Series
GS-511 - Auditing Series
GS-512 - Internal Revenue Agent Series
GS-525 - Accounting Technician Series
GS-526 - Tax Specialist Series
GS-530 - Cash Processing Series
GS-540 - Voucher Examining Series
GS-544 - Civilian Pay Series
GS-545 - Military Pay Series
GS-560 - Budget Analysis Series
GS-561 - Budget Clerical and Assistance Series
GS-592 - Tax Examining Series
GS-593 - Insurance Accounts Series
GS-599 - Financial Management Student Trainee Series

GS-600 – MEDICAL, HOSPITAL, DENTAL, AND PUBLIC HEALTH GROUP

This group includes all classes of positions the duties of which are to advise on, administer, supervise or perform research or other professional and scientific work, subordinate technical work, or related clerical work in the several branches of medicine, surgery, and dentistry or in related patient care services such as dietetics, nursing, occupational therapy, physical therapy, pharmacy, and others.

Series in this group are:
GS-601 - General Health Science Series
GS-602 - Medical Officer Series
GS-603 - Physician's Assistant Series
GS-610 - Nurse Series
GS-620 - Practical Nurse Series
GS-621 - Nursing Assistant Series
GS-622 - Medical Supply Aide and Technician Series
GS-625 - Autopsy Assistant Series
GS-630 - Dietitian and Nutritionist Series
GS-631 - Occupational Therapist Series
GS-633 - Physical Therapist Series
GS-635 - Kinesiotherapy Series
GS-636 - Rehabilitation Therapy Assistant Series
GS-637 - Manual Arts Therapist Series
GS-638 - Recreation/Creative Arts Therapist Series
GS-639 - Educational Therapist Series
GS-640 - Health Aid and Technician Series
GS-642 - Nuclear Medicine Technician Series
GS-644 - Medical Technologist Series
GS-645 - Medical Technician Series
GS-646 - Pathology Technician Series
GS-647 - Diagnostic Radiologic Technologist Series
GS-648 - Therapeutic Radiologic Technologist Series
GS-649 - Medical Instrument Technician Series
GS-650 - Medical Technical Assistant Series
GS-651 - Respiratory Therapist Series
GS-660 - Pharmacist Series
GS-661 - Pharmacy Technician Series
GS-662 - Optometrist Series
GS-664 - Restoration Technician Series
GS-665 - Speech Pathology and Audiology Series
GS-667 - Orthotist and Prosthetist Series
GS-668 - Podiatrist Series
GS-669 - Medical Records Administration Series
GS-670 - Health System Administration Series
GS-671 - Health System Specialist Series
GS-672 - Prosthetic Representative Series
GS-673 - Hospital Housekeeping Management

Series
GS-675 - Medical Records Technician Series
GS-679 - Medical Support Assistance Series
GS-680 - Dental Officer Series
GS-681 - Dental Assistant Series
GS-682 - Dental Hygiene Series
GS-683 - Dental Laboratory Aid and Technician
        Series
GS-685 - Public Health Program Specialist Series
GS-688 - Sanitarian Series
GS-690 - Industrial Hygiene Series
GS-696 - Consumer Safety Series
GS-698 - Environmental Health Technician Series
GS-699 - Medical and Health Student Trainee
        Series

GS-700 - VETERINARY MEDICAL SCIENCE GROUP

This group includes positions that advise on, administer, supervise, or perform professional or technical support work in the various branches of veterinary medical science.

Series in this group are:
GS-701 - Veterinary Medical Science Series
GS-704 - Animal Health Technician Series
GS-799 - Veterinary Student Trainee Series

GS-800 – ENGINEERING AND ARCHITECTURE GROUP

This group includes all classes of positions the duties of which are to advise on, administer, supervise, or perform professional, scientific, or technical work concerned with engineering or architectural projects, facilities, structures, systems, processes, equipment, devices, materials or methods. Positions in this group require knowledge of the science or art, or both, by which materials, natural resources, and power are made useful.

Series in this group are:
GS-801 - General Engineering Series
GS-802 - Engineering Technician Series
GS-803 - Safety Engineering Series
GS-804 - Fire Protection Engineering Series
GS-806 - Materials Engineering Series
GS-807 - Landscape Architecture Series
GS-808 - Architecture Series
GS-809 - Construction Control Technical Series
GS-810 - Civil Engineering Series

GS-817 - Survey Technical Series
GS-819 - Environmental Engineering Series
GS-828 - Construction Analyst Series
GS-830 - Mechanical Engineering Series
GS-840 - Nuclear Engineering Series
GS-850 - Electrical Engineering Series
GS-854 - Computer Engineering Series
GS-855 - Electronics Engineering Series
GS-856 - Electronics Technical Series
GS-858 - Biomedical Engineering Series
GS-861 - Aerospace Engineering Series
GS-871 - Naval Architecture Series
GS-873 - Marine Survey Technical Series
GS-880 - Mining Engineering Series
GS-881 - Petroleum Engineering Series
GS-890 - Agricultural Engineering Series
GS-892 - Ceramic Engineering Series
GS-893 - Chemical Engineering Series
GS-894 - Welding Engineering Series
GS-895 - Industrial Engineering Technical Series
GS-896 - Industrial Engineering Series
GS-899 - Engineering and Architecture Student
        Trainee Series

GS-900 – LEGAL AND KINDRED GROUP

This group includes all positions that advise on, administer, supervise, or perform work of a legal or kindred nature.

Series in this group are:
GS-901 - General Legal and Kindred Administration
        Series
GS-904 - Law Clerk Series
GS-905 - General Attorney Series
GS-920 - Estate Tax Examining Series
GS-930 - Hearings and Appeals Series
GS-945 - Clerk of Court Series
GS-950 - Paralegal Specialist Series
GS-958 - Employee Benefits Law Series
GS-962 - Contact Representative Series
GS-963 - Legal Instruments Examining Series
GS-965 - Land Law Examining Series
GS-967 - Passport and Visa Examining Series
GS-986 - Legal Assistance Series
GS-987 - Tax Law Specialist Series
GS-991 - Workers' Compensation Claims Examining
        Series
GS-993 - Railroad Retirement Claims Examining
        Series
GS-996 - Veterans Claims Examining Series
GS-998 - Claims Assistance and Examining Series
GS-999 - Legal Occupations Student Trainee Series

GS-1000 – INFORMATION AND ARTS GROUP

This group includes positions which involve professional, artistic, technical, or clerical work in (1) the communication of information and ideas through verbal, visual, or pictorial means, (2) the collection, custody, presentation, display, and interpretation of art works, cultural objects, and other artifacts, or (3) a branch of fine or applied arts such as industrial design, interior design, or musical composition. Positions in this group require writing, editing, and language ability; artistic skill and ability; knowledge of foreign languages; the ability to evaluate and interpret informational and cultural materials; or the practical application of technical or esthetic principles combined with manual skill and dexterity; or related clerical skills.

Series in this group are:
GS-1001 - General Arts and Information Series
GS-1008 - Interior Design Series
GS-1010 - Exhibits Specialist Series
GS-1015 - Museum Curator Series
GS-1016 - Museum Specialist and Technician
Series
GS-1020 - Illustrating Series
GS-1021 - Office Drafting Series
GS-1035 - Public Affairs Series
GS-1040 - Language Specialist Series
GS-1046 - Language Clerical Series
GS-1051 - Music Specialist Series
GS-1054 - Theater Specialist Series
GS-1056 - Art Specialist Series
GS-1060 - Photography Series
GS-1071 - Audiovisual Production Series
GS-1082 - Writing and Editing Series
GS-1083 - Technical Writing and Editing Series
GS-1084 - Visual Information Series
GS-1087 - Editorial Assistance Series
GS-1099 - Information and Arts Student Trainee
Series

GS-1100 – BUSINESS AND INDUSTRY GROUP

This group includes all classes of positions the duties of which are to advise on, administer, supervise, or perform work pertaining to and requiring a knowledge of business and trade practices, characteristics and use of equipment, products, or property, or industrial production methods and processes, including the conduct of investigations and studies; the collection, analysis, and dissemination of information; the establishment and maintenance of contacts with industry and commerce; the provision of advisory services; the examination and appraisement of merchandise or property; and the administration of regulatory provisions and controls.

Series in this group are:
GS-1101 - General Business and Industry Series
GS-1102 - Contracting Series
GS-1103 - Industrial Property Management Series
GS-1104 - Property Disposal Series
GS-1105 - Purchasing Series
GS-1106 - Procurement Clerical and Technician
Series
GS-1107 - Property Disposal Clerical and
Technician Series
GS-1130 - Public Utilities Specialist Series
GS-1140 - Trade Specialist Series
GS-1144 - Commissary Management Series
GS-1145 - Agricultural Program Specialist Series
GS-1146 - Agricultural Marketing Series
GS-1147 - Agricultural Market Reporting Series
GS-1150 - Industrial Specialist Series
GS-1152 - Production Control Series
GS-1160 - Financial Analysis Series
GS-1163 - Insurance Examining Series
GS-1165 - Loan Specialist Series
GS-1169 - Internal Revenue Officer Series
GS-1170 - Realty Series
GS-1171 - Appraising Series
GS-1173 - Housing Management Series
GS-1176 - Building Management Series
GS-1199 - Business and Industry Student Trainee
Series

GS-1200 – COPYRIGHT, PATENT, AND TRADEMARK GROUP

This group includes all classes of positions the duties of which are to advise on, administer, supervise, or perform professional scientific, technical, and legal work involved in the cataloging and registration of copyrights, in the classification and issuance of patents, in the registration of trademarks, in the prosecution of applications for patents before the Patent Office, and in the giving of advice to Government officials on patent matters.

Series in this group are:
GS-1202 - Patent Technician Series
GS-1210 - Copyright Series

GS-1220 - Patent Administration Series
GS-1221 - Patent Adviser Series
GS-1222 - Patent Attorney Series
GS-1223 - Patent Classifying Series
GS-1224 - Patent Examining Series
GS-1226 - Design Patent Examining Series
GS-1299 - Copyright and Patent Student Trainee Series

GS-1300 – PHYSICAL SCIENCES GROUP

This group includes all classes of positions the duties of which are to advise on, administer, supervise, or perform research or other professional and scientific work or subordinate technical work in any of the fields of science concerned with matter, energy, physical space, time, nature of physical measurement, and fundamental structural particles; and the nature of the physical environment.

Series in this group are:
GS-1301 - General Physical Science Series
GS-1306 - Health Physics Series
GS-1310 - Physics Series
GS-1311 - Physical Science Technician Series
GS-1313 - Geophysics Series
GS-1315 - Hydrology Series
GS-1316 - Hydrologic Technician Series
GS-1320 - Chemistry Series
GS-1321 - Metallurgy Series
GS-1330 - Astronomy and Space Science Series
GS-1340 - Meteorology Series
GS-1341 - Meteorological Technician Series
GS-1350 - Geology Series
GS-1360 - Oceanography Series
GS-1361 - Navigational Information Series
GS-1370 - Cartography Series
GS-1371 - Cartographic Technician Series
GS-1372 - Geodesy Series
GS-1373 - Land Surveying Series
GS-1374 - Geodetic Technician Series
GS-1380 - Forest Products Technology Series
GS-1382 - Food Technology Series
GS-1384 - Textile Technology Series
GS-1386 - Photographic Technology Series
GS-1397 - Document Analysis Series
GS-1399 - Physical Science Student Trainee Series

GS-1400 – LIBRARY AND ARCHIVES GROUP

This group includes all classes of positions the duties of which are to advise on, administer, supervise, or perform professional and scientific work or subordinate technical work in the various phases of library and archival science.

Series in this group are:
GS-1410 - Librarian Series
GS-1411 - Library Technician Series
GS-1412 - Technical Information Services Series
GS-1420 - Archivist Series
GS-1421 - Archives Technician Series
GS-1499 - Library and Archives Student Trainee Series

GS-1500 – MATHEMATICS AND STATISTICS GROUP

This group includes all classes of positions the duties of which are to advise on, administer, supervise, or perform professional and scientific work or related clerical work in basic mathematical principles, methods, procedures, or relationships, including the development and application of mathematical methods for the investigation and solution of problems; the development and application of statistical theory in the selection, collection, classification, adjustment, analysis, and interpretation of data; the development and application of mathematical, statistical, and financial principles to programs or problems involving life and property risks; and any other professional and scientific or related clerical work requiring primarily and mainly the understanding and use of mathematical theories, methods, and operations.

Series in this group are:
GS-1501 - General Mathematics and Statistics Series
GS-1510 - Actuarial Science Series
GS-1515 - Operations Research Series
GS-1520 - Mathematics Series
GS-1521 - Mathematics Technician Series
GS-1529 - Mathematical Statistics Series
GS-1530 - Statistics Series
GS-1531 - Statistical Assistant Series
GS-1540 - Cryptography Series
GS-1541 - Cryptanalysis Series
GS-1550 - Computer Science Series
GS-1599 - Mathematics and Statistics Student Trainee Series

GS-1600 – EQUIPMENT, FACILITIES, AND SERVICES GROUP

This group includes positions the duties of which are to advise on, manage, or provide instructions and information concerning the operation, maintenance, and use of equipment, shops, buildings, laundries, printing plants, power plants, cemeteries, or other government facilities, or other work involving services provided predominantly by persons in trades. Positions in this group require technical or managerial knowledge and ability, plus a practical knowledge of trades, crafts, or manual labor operations.

Series in this group are:
GS-1601 - Equipment, Facilities, and Services Series
GS-1603 - Equipment, Facilities, and Services Assistance Series
GS-1630 - Cemetery Administration Services Series
GS-1640 - Facility Operations Services Series
GS-1654 - Printing Services Series
GS-1658 - Laundry Operations Services Series
GS-1667 - Food Services Series
GS-1670 - Equipment Services Series
GS-1699 - Equipment, Facilities, and Services Student Trainee Series

GS-1700 – EDUCATION GROUP

This group includes positions that involve administering, managing, supervising, performing, or supporting education or training work when the paramount requirement of the position is knowledge of, or skill in, education, training, or instruction processes.

Series in this group are:
GS-1701 - General Education and Training Series
GS-1702 - Education and Training Technician Series
GS-1710 - Education and Vocational Training Series
GS-1712 - Training Instruction Series
GS-1715 - Vocational Rehabilitation Series
GS-1720 - Education Program Series
GS-1725 - Public Health Educator Series
GS-1730 - Education Research Series
GS-1740 - Education Services Series
GS-1750 - Instructional Systems Series
GS-1799 - Education Student Trainee Series

GS-1800 – INVESTIGATION GROUP

This group includes all classes of positions the duties of which are to advise on, administer, supervise, or perform investigation, inspection, or enforcement work primarily concerned with alleged or suspected offenses against the laws of the United States, or such work primarily concerned with determining compliance with laws and regulations.

Series in this group are:
GS-1801 - General Inspection, Investigation, and Compliance Series
GS-1802 - Compliance Inspection and Support Series
GS-1810 - General Investigating Series
GS-1811 - Criminal Investigating Series
GS-1812 - Game Law Enforcement Series
GS-1815 - Air Safety Investigating Series
GS-1816 - Immigration Inspection Series
GS-1822 - Mine Safety and Health Series
GS-1825 - Aviation Safety Series
GS-1831 - Securities Compliance Examining Series
GS-1850 - Agricultural Commodity Warehouse Examining Series
GS-1854 - Alcohol, Tobacco and Firearms Inspection Series
GS-1862 - Consumer Safety Inspection Series
GS-1863 - Food Inspection Series
GS-1864 - Public Health Quarantine Inspection Series
GS-1881 - Customs and Border Protection Interdiction Series
GS-1884 - Customs Patrol Officer Series
GS-1889 - Import Specialist Series
GS-1890 - Customs Inspection Series
GS-1894 - Customs Entry and Liquidating Series
GS-1895 - Customs and Border Protection Series
GS-1896 - Border Patrol Agent Series
GS-1897 - Customs Aid Series
GS-1899 - Investigation Student Trainee Series

GS-1900 – QUALITY ASSURANCE, INSPECTION, AND GRADING GROUP

This group includes all classes of positions the duties of which are advise on, supervise, or perform administrative or technical work primarily concerned with the quality assurance or inspection of material, facilities, and processes; or with the grading of commodities under official standards.

Series in this group are:
GS-1910 - Quality Assurance Series
GS-1980 - Agricultural Commodity Grading Series
GS-1981 - Agricultural Commodity Aid Series
GS-1999 - Quality Inspection Student Trainee Series

GS-2000 – SUPPLY GROUP

This group includes positions that involve work concerned with furnishing all types of supplies, equipment, material, property (except real estate), and certain services to components of the federal government, industrial, or other concerns under contract to the government, or receiving supplies from the federal government. Included are positions concerned with one or more aspects of supply activities from initial planning, including requirements analysis and determination, through acquisition, cataloging, storage, distribution, utilization to ultimate issues for consumption or disposal. The work requires a knowledge of one or more elements or parts of a supply system, and/or supply methods, policies, or procedures.

Series in this group are:
GS-2001 - General Supply Series
GS-2003 - Supply Program Management Series
GS-2005 - Supply Clerical and Technician Series
GS-2010 - Inventory Management Series
GS-2030 - Distribution Facilities and Storage Management Series
GS-2032 - Packaging Series
GS-2050 - Supply Cataloging Series
GS-2091 - Sales Store Clerical Series
GS-2099 - Supply Student Trainee Series

GS-2100 – TRANSPORTATION GROUP

This group includes all classes of positions the duties of which are to advise on, administer, supervise, or perform clerical, administrative, or technical work involved in the provision of transportation service to the government, the regulation of transportation utilities by the government, or the management of government-funded transportation programs, including transportation research and development projects.

Series in this group are:
GS-2101 - Transportation Specialist Series
GS-2102 - Transportation Clerk and Assistant Series
GS-2110 - Transportation Industry Analysis Series
GS-2121 - Railroad Safety Series
GS-2123 - Motor Carrier Safety Series
GS-2125 - Highway Safety Series
GS-2130 - Traffic Management Series
GS-2131 - Freight Rate Series
GS-2135 - Transportation Loss and Damage Claims Examining Series
GS-2144 - Cargo Scheduling Series
GS-2150 - Transportation Operations Series
GS-2151 - Dispatching Series
GS-2152 - Air Traffic Control Series
GS-2154 - Air Traffic Assistance Series
GS-2161 - Marine Cargo Series
GS-2181 - Aircraft Operation Series
GS-2183 - Air Navigation Series
GS-2185 - Aircrew Technician Series
GS-2199 - Transportation Student Trainee Series

GS-2200 – INFORMATION TECHNOLOGY GROUP

Series in this group are:
GS-2210 - Information Technology Management Series
GS-2299 - Information Technology Student Trainee series

TRADES, CRAFTS, AND LABOR POSITIONS | STEP 1

Federal Classification and Job Grading Systems

▸ Main ▸ White Collar Positions	Job Grading Standards for Trades, Craft, and Labor Positions

www.opm.gov/fedclass/html/fwseries.asp

2500 Wire Communications Equipment Installation and Maintenance Group
2600 Electronic Equipment Installation and Maintenance Group
2800 Electrical Installation and Maintenance Group
3100 Fabric and Leather Work Group
3300 Instrument Work Group
3400 Machine Tool Work Group
3500 General Services and Support Work Group
3600 Structural and Finishing Work Group
3700 Metal Processing Group
3800 Metal Work Group
3900 Motion Picture, Radio, Television, and Sound Equipment Operating Group
4100 Painting and Paperhanging Group
4200 Plumbing and Pipefitting Group
4300 Pliable Materials Work Group
4400 Printing Group
4600 Wood Work Group
4700 General Maintenance and Operations Work Group
4800 General Equipment Maintenance Group
5000 Plant and Animal Work Group
5200 Miscellaneous Occupations Group
5300 Industrial Equipment Maintenance Group
5400 Industrial Equipment Operation Group
5700 Transportation/Mobile Equipment Operation Group
5800 Transportation/Mobile Equipment Maintenance Group
6500 Ammunition, Explosives, and Toxic Materials Work Group
6600 Armament Work Group
6900 Warehousing and Stock Handling Group
7000 Packing and Processing Group
7300 Laundry, Dry Cleaning, and Pressing Group
7400 Food Preparation and Serving Group
7600 Personal Services Group
8200 Fluid Systems Maintenance Group
8600 Engine Overhaul Group
8800 Aircraft Overhaul Group

The Human Resources staffing specialist will determine your qualifications for the position by looking at the following items in your federal resume. Qualification determinations are based on:

EXPERIENCE
➤ Quality of experience
  • Directly related to the job or general nature of work
  • Complexity of assignments (what, for whom, why)
  • Decision-making authority or span of control
  • Knowledge, skills, and abilities used
➤ Length of experience
  • Full-time or part-time
  • Number of hours per week

EDUCATION
➤ Major field of study
➤ Number of years completed or number of semester hours completed
➤ GPA

TRAINING
➤ Related to job
➤ # of days or hours

Qualifying Based on Education Alone

GS-2: High school graduation or equivalent (i.e., GED)

GS-3: One year above high school

GS-4: Two years above high school (or Associate's degree)

GS-5: Bachelor's degree

GS 7: One full year of graduate study or Bachelor's degree with superior academic achievement (GPA 2.95 or higher out of a possible 4.0)

GS-9: Master's degree or equivalent such as J.D. or LL.B.

GS-11: Ph.D.

NOTE: There are exceptions to this chart; there are occupations that will not accept education in lieu of experience.

MILITARY RANK TO FEDERAL CIVILIAN GRADES |

Determining the government grade level based on your military rank is challenging. Here are some ways to determine the appropriate grade:

- **Salary:** Match the salary you are earning now against the OPM General Schedule charts.

- **Specialized Experience:** Read USAJOBS announcements for the Specialized Experience required and see if you qualify for the grade level they are advertising.

- **Certification and Training**: Read job announcements and see if you have the specific certification and training required.

NOTE: The chart below is not an official federal government grade to military rank conversion chart. This chart was developed out of years of analyzing rank against the requirements of USAJOBS vacancy announcements for specific positions. Grade levels for these roles may differ based on an agency's organizational structure, geographical location, and/or size.

Federal Civilian Grade	Military Commissioned Officer	Military Warrant Officer	Military Enlisted
Assistants			Trainee/Assistants
GS-2, 3,4,5			E-2,3,4
6,7,8			E-5,6
Specialist/Technician	Junior Leaders / First-line Supervisors		Specialist/ First-line Supervisors
GS-7			E-3,4
9	O-1		E-5, E-7
11	2	WO-1	E-5, E-7
12	3	WO-1	E-7
Team Lead/ Section Leader	Mid-level Leader/ Section Manager		Operations Supervisor/ Supervisor of First-line Supervisors
GS-12	O-3, 4	WO-2	E-7, 8
13	4	3	E-8
Supervisor/ Branch Chief	Leader of Mid-Level Leaders /Manage Organizations		Superintendent/ Supervisor of Ops Supervisors
GS-13	O-4	WO-4	E-8, 9
14	5	5	E-9
Manager	Senior Leader / Head of Organization		Senior Enl Advisor/ Career Field Manager
GS-14	O-5	WO-5	
15	6		

2015 GENERAL SCHEDULE

Effective January 2015 – Annual Rates by Grade and Step

https://www.opm.gov/policy-data-oversight/pay-leave/salaries-wages/2015/general-schedule/

The General Schedule (GS) is a worldwide pay system that covers more than 1.5 million employees. The GS pay schedule has 15 grades and 10 steps in each grade covering more than 400 occupations. Pay varies by geographic location.

TIP: Be sure to look up your potential salary WITH your locality pay!
- Washington, DC / Baltimore: Add **24.22%** to base salary
- San Diego, CA: Add **24.19%** to base salary
- Hawaii: Add **16.51%** to base salary

Grade	Step 1	Step 2	Step 3	Step 4	Step 5	Step 6	Step 7	Step 8	Step 9	Step 10	Within Grade
1	18161	18768	19372	19973	20577	20931	21528	22130	22153	22712	VARIES
2	20419	20905	21581	22153	22403	23062	23721	24380	25039	25698	VARIES
3	22279	23022	23765	24508	25251	25994	26737	27480	28223	28966	743
4	25011	25845	26679	27513	28347	29181	30015	30849	31683	32517	834
5	27982	28915	29848	30781	31714	32647	33580	34513	35446	36379	933
6	31192	32232	33272	34312	35352	36392	37432	38472	39512	40552	1040
7	34662	35817	36972	38127	39282	40437	41592	42747	43902	45057	1155
8	38387	39667	40947	42227	43507	44787	46067	47347	48627	49907	1280
9	42399	43812	45225	46638	48051	49464	50877	52290	53703	55116	1413
10	46691	48247	49803	51359	52915	54471	56027	57583	59139	60695	1556
11	51298	53008	54718	56428	58138	59848	61558	63268	64978	66688	1710
12	61486	63536	65586	67636	69686	71736	73786	75836	77886	79936	2050
13	73115	75552	77989	80426	82863	85300	87737	90174	92611	95048	2437
14	86399	89279	92159	95039	97919	100799	103679	106559	109439	112319	2880
15	101630	105018	108406	111794	115182	118570	121958	125346	128734	132122	3388

Now that we have covered the basic General Schedule grade and pay system, we'll tell you that not every agency follows this pay system anymore. "Pay banding," which allows an organization to combine two or more grades into a wider "band," is an increasingly popular alternative to the traditional GS system. The "grade" information for jobs in agencies using pay banding will have a different look, and that look may be specific to a particular agency. Don't be surprised to see something as odd as ZP-1 or NO-2 in place of GS-5 or GS-7. Focus on the duties, the salary, whether you are qualified for the job, and whether you would like to have it. Remember, the federal government is large, and needs a way to increase flexibility of pay based on performance. Pay bands are its answer.

Example of Pay Band Salaries: Transportation Security Administration

http://www.tsa.gov/careers/pay-bands

Pay Band	Minimum	Maximum
A	$17,427	$25,479
B	$19,964	$29,119
C	$22,613	$33,972
D	$26,031	$39,047
E	$29,891	$44,891
F	$34,303	$51,509
G	$40,150	$62,208
H	$48,972	$75,885
I	$59,671	$92,540
J	$72,799	$112,835
K	$87,026	$134,895
L	$104,012	$158,700
M	$121,438	$158,700

STEP 2

Network– Who Do You Know?

Why Network?

The U.S. federal government employs nearly two million people in civilian jobs, making it the biggest employer in the country. Understandably, the hiring system can sometimes be complex and daunting. Networking is a great opportunity to learn about the federal hiring system. Other people, especially current and former federal employees, are often the best source of basic information and insider tips.

Who Do You Know and Why Is It Important?

Do you know a supervisor at an agency or a military base? It's possible that veterans could get hired by this supervisor. The Veterans Recruitment Appointment (VRA) offers special hiring programs for retiring and separating military (disabled or non-disabled). VRA gives supervisors the authority to make direct hires in the case of veterans, but even under direct hiring, the jobseeker must submit an application.

Contact List

Make a list of federal employee contacts and keep their information handy for networking.

Name of person:

Agency where he/she works:

Location:

Job title:

What does he/she do in the government?

CAREER EXPOS FOR MILITARY PERSONNEL

One of the best places to learn about federal jobs, agencies, and opportunities is at a military career expo. On occasion, the federal Human Resources specialist may even bring along a few direct hire opportunities for government positions or internships. Have your resume ready to hand out. Your federal resume should feature your most relevant skills for easy reading and review by the Human Resources recruiters. Also, practice the job fair script before you go.

Job Fair Script

Prepare your own job fair script here. Practice your script with a friend.

Hello, my name is: _____

Where are you from? _____

Military service: _____
_____

Recent activity: _____
What was involved in that? _____
What was the result of that activity? _____
What was your role? _____

What kind of job are you looking for? _____
_____
_____

What are your basic skills? _____
_____
_____

Where do you want to live now? _____
_____
_____

NETWORKING / CAREER EXPO RESUME (MILITARY)

Intrroducting Dan Low: Separated as 30% or more disabled veteran (CPS) as USMC Rifleman; attended college on GI Bill; got a BS in criminology; wanted a job as FBI Special Agent; landed an internship with IRS while he waits for Special Agent position.

DAN LOW
1234 Murphy Lane | Philadelphia, PA 19104
555-123-4567 | danlow@yahoo.com

Veterans' Preference: 30% or More Disabled, E-5, USMC 2006-2012, Purple Heart Recipient

---

SKILLS SUMMARY

Criminal Justice • Military Security • Physical Security • Combat Operations • Search Operations • Team Leadership • Interpersonal Communication
Languages: Korean and English

EDUCATION

BACHELOR OF SCIENCE
Rosemont College • Rosemont, PA • May 2015
Major: Criminal Justice • GPA: 3.70

ASSOCIATE OF SCIENCE
Delaware County Community College • Media, PA • June 2013
Major: Criminal Justice • GPA: 3.60 • Phi Theta Kappa Honors

UNDERGRADUATE COURSEWORK
West Chester University • West Chester, PA • 2012-2013
Major: Criminal Justice • GPA: 3.0

PROFESSIONAL EXPERIENCE

Security Assistant (Intern)   01/2015 – Present
Internal Revenue Service   Salary: Volunteer
Philadelphia, PA 19104   Hours per week: 25
Supervisor: Michael Hoffman (987-654-3210)

- PHYSICAL SECURITY: Implement physical security procedures, processes, and techniques in support of protecting a Level-4 security building. Conduct surveillance and foot patrols. Check locks, alarms, and other barriers. Respond to security incidents and emergencies within the building. Conduct investigations of incidents.

- SECURITY CONTROL: Control the movement of persons around and in the building. Verify personal identification against authorization documents and check badges of personnel requesting access to the building. Prepare and issue identification cards.

- EFFECTIVE COMMUNICATION: Brief employees and visitors on building access controls and restrictions. Conduct trainings concerning security issues and restrictions. Coordinate with guards and Federal police during incident response.

Rifleman
Marine Corps, 2nd Battalion
Kaneohe Bay, HI • Baghdad, Iraq
Supervisor: Capt. Thomas Jefferson (123-456-7890)

09/2006 – 07/2012
Rank: Lance Corporal
Salary: $45,000 per year
Hours per week: 40+

Deployed to the Haditha Triad, Iraq, in support of Operation Iraqi Freedom.

- LEADERSHIP: Supervised and motivated Marines in combat, ensuring mission success and troop welfare. Led a team of four soldiers on mounted security patrols. Organized and planned security around Iraqi check points to search vehicles for weapons.

- SECURITY MANAGEMENT: Served as a primary scout, responsible for front line security. Provided foot and mobilized patrols of control points and the forward operating base. Transported criminally accused Marines to military jail and to military trials.

- COMBAT OPERATIONS: Served as rifleman with assault troops and close combat forces. Conducted offensive tactics in confined spaces. Participated in dozens of combat patrols, made life and death decisions, and managed complex battlefield operations.

- SEARCH OPERATIONS: Conducted patrols and searches for high value target terrorists and improvised explosive devices. Conducted house searches based on intelligence and detained known or suspected terrorists.

- TRAINING & COMMUNICATIONS: Worked as part of a team that led rigorous training program to train and teach Iraqi police personnel how to use U.S. weapons and tactics. Interacted with civilians promoting cooperation and good will.

Accomplishments: Awarded the Purple Heart in 2007 for being wounded in a firefight while posting security for a Marine to cross a long open field. Awarded Combat Action Ribbon in recognition of having participated under enemy fire in ground combat fire-fight action.

TRAINING

Military Academic Skills Program, 140 clock hours, 11/2008 • Marine Rifleman: Combat Skills, Marine Corps Institute, 9/2007 • Land Navigation, Marine Corps Institute, 9/2007 • Infantry Patrolling, Marine Corps Institute, 7/2007 • Fundamentals of Marine Corps Leadership, Marine Corps Institute, 6/2006 • Infantry Rifleman, Infantry School, 3/2006 • Marine Recruit Training Boot Camp, 09/2005

CERTIFICATIONS

Combat Water Surface Survival, U.S. Marine Corps, 08/2007 • Advanced Aircraft Ditching, U.S. Marine Corps, 8/2007 • IPHABD Qualification, U.S. Marine Corps, 8/2007 • Basic Aircraft Ditching, U.S. Marine Corps, 8/2007 • Surface Survival, U.S. Marine Corps, 8/2007 • First Aid and CPR/AED, American Red Cross, 12/2012

COMMUNITY SERVICE

Small Group Leader, Church Korean Ministry, Feb 2013 – June 2013 • Vice President, Church Korean Ministry Leader July 2009 – July 2011

NETWORKING / JOB FAIR RESUME (FAMILY MEMBER)

ANESHA T. GAFFNEY

PSC 999 Box 11, Rota, Spain, FPO, AE, 09634
666.666.6666
Email: anesha.gaffney@yahoo.com

Family Member of USN Active Duty
Eligible for Consideration under Executive Order 13473, September 11, 2009

SUMMARY OF SKILLS:

Instructor, Adult Educator
Program Developer and Coordinator
Mentor and Coach, Community Liaison
Administration, Writing and Computer Skills
Public Speaker and Speaking Coach

HIGHLIGHTS OF EXPERIENCE:

- ***Family readiness and quality of life support:*** career advisor, relocation counselor, and referrals for needed services for USN family members in Rota.
- ***Provided adult education, instruction, and training*** at University of West Florida, and increased operational readiness.
- ***Coordinated and supervised*** first Annual Northwest Florida Districts High School Speech Tournament.
- ***Community liaison*** establishing a network for the University of West Florida and N.A.S. Pensacola.
- ***President's Award for Leadership and Diversity,*** Univ. of W. FL (2008).
- ***Proficient in Microsoft Office programs,*** Windows Movie Maker, Final Cut Pro, and iMovie. ***Typing Speed 60 wpm.***

WORK EXPERIENCE:

Fleet and Family Support Center, US Navy, Rota, Spain
Volunteer, 8/2010 – Present, 20 hours per week

• INFORMATION AND REFERRAL: Identified and clarified issues or concerns and determined appropriate referral services for military members, retirees, and family members. Ensured customer service and satisfaction.
• CUSTOMER SERVICE: Primary contact for department and ensured and delivered services to customers including educating clients on Relocation Services and Career Resource Development.
• MARKETING: Gathered data for Fleet and Family Support Center and updated information for department calendar and for NAVSTA Rota advertisement.
• DATA GATHERING: Utilized Microsoft Office software to compile and report information and statistics for use at the installation.

University of West Florida, Tampa, FL

Graduate Assistant Coach, 8/2008 to 5/2010, 30 hours per week

• INSTRUCTOR AND COACH. Designed training structure and determined appropriate alternative routes to more effective coaching techniques.
-- Over 5,000 hours of coaching students in effective writing and presentation skills.

• RECRUITER. Made recommendations for University of West Florida Forensics Team. Community liaison for team.
-- Created promotional DVDs; coordinated external events on campus to recruit on-campus students. Coordinated with Director of Forensics with national and regional travel plans for approximately 10 students.

EDUCATION:

Master of Science, Public Administration, 2010
University of West Florida, Pensacola, FL
Financial Management, Public Budgeting
Public Service Human Resources Management
Conflict Management & Resolution, Marketing Management

Bachelor of Arts in Organizational Communications, 2008
University of West Florida, Pensacola, FL

- Leadership Communications (Project Car-A-Van) - raised funds to purchase 15-passenger van for Ronald McDonald House of Northwest Florida (2006).
- Health Communications (Project KidCare) - Worked with Florida KidCare to raise awareness of medical insurance to families of lower socioeconomic status (2008).

HONORS

- Outstanding Graduate Student Award, University of West Florida (2010)
  Recipient of Letter of Appreciation from Commanding Officer for Volunteer Service, N.A.S. Pensacola (2009)
- President's Award for Leadership and Diversity, University of West Florida (2008)
- Four-time National Finalist: 2008 Pi Kappa Delta National Speech and Debate Championship Finalist (2005-2008)
- Top 24 collegiate speaker in the US in multiple categories, National Forensic Association (2008)
- Volunteer Shining Star Award, Ronald McDonald House of Northwest Florida (2007)

STEP 2 | LINKEDIN NETWORKING

Life is about relationships, and LinkedIn has opened the door to help build more relationships worldwide.

LinkedIn, with 250 million professionals in its network, is THE business channel for recruiting.

However, it is also so much more. LinkedIn provides an opportunity to build a worldwide network of professionals who can assist you with your career. Not only does it work for military to civilian transitions, it also works within the military framework where military to military assignments are concerned. Many military members have made connections for their next military assignment with another military professional using LinkedIn. LinkedIn can be regarded as a marvelous "networking" tool, though it should not be used as a substitute for good old-fashioned relationship building.

LinkedIn is a great tool for military spouses for PCS moves.

Before LinkedIn, it was very difficult to build a professional network outside of your current assignment. With the worldwide network that LinkedIn provides, military spouses are now able to build a professional network online.

Whether it is a short notice PCS move, a change in PCS orders, or a normal PCS rotation, or even in the case of a service member's extended or remote tours of duty (deployment etc.), military spouses can build strong professional networks via LinkedIn.

Fast updates to your network (and their network) for frequent moves!

With the ability of LinkedIn to share the same message with 50 of your contacts at a click of the button, it will not take long to inform your entire contact list of any changes in your business and professional circumstance. Each of your contacts will also have other contacts who will be able to refer you to positions, whether you are simply looking for a change or moving due to a military assignment.

Employers expect to find professionals on LinkedIn.

Many of our clients report that their LinkedIn profile was reviewed prior to their interview by the interviewers. This situation works fabulously both ways. The interviewer will have a great impression of you if you have done your work on LinkedIn, and you can research the interviewer prior to your interview.

The LinkedIn resume for Natalie Richardson on the facing page was developed based on her federal resume.

We added an exciting profile with her most outstanding skills. LinkedIn is a professional place where you can post a photograph and introduce your strengths, mission, and career history to an employer or network. You can even ask for recommendations from your best customers or team members who will write about your strengths and accomplishments.

Did You Know?

Business professionals and Human Resources managers use LinkedIn to check out potential job candidates. Individuals with more than 20 connections are **34 times** more likely to be approached with a job opportunity.

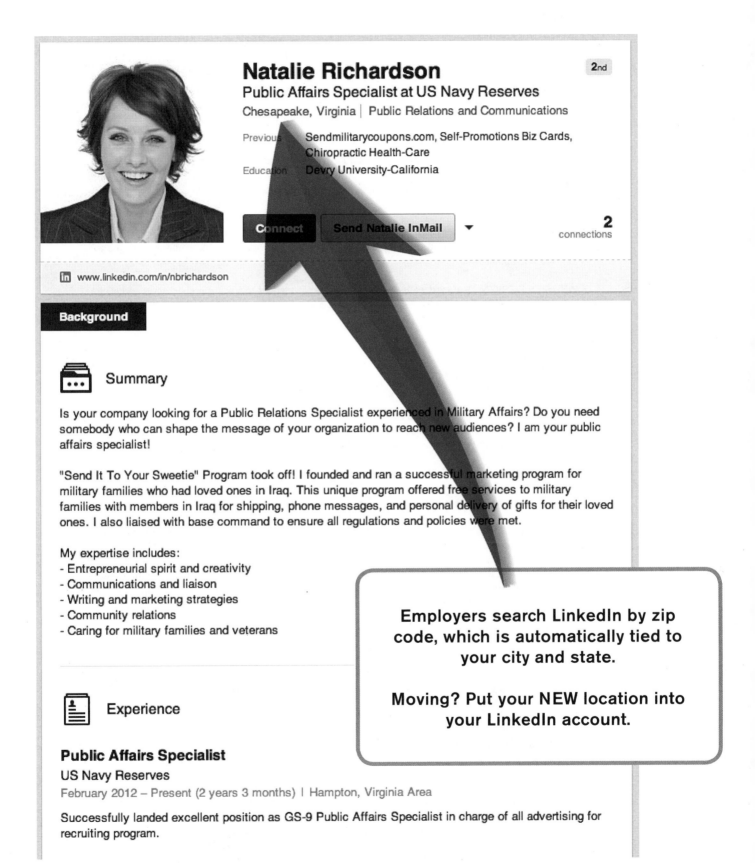

Natalie Richardson 2nd

Public Affairs Specialist at US Navy Reserves

Chesapeake, Virginia | Public Relations and Communications

Previous Sendmilitarycoupons.com, Self-Promotions Biz Cards, Chiropractic Health-Care

Education Devry University-California

[Connect] [Send Natalie InMail] ▼

2
connections

in www.linkedin.com/in/nbrichardson

Background

Summary

Is your company looking for a Public Relations Specialist experienced in Military Affairs? Do you need somebody who can shape the message of your organization to reach new audiences? I am your public affairs specialist!

"Send It To Your Sweetie" Program took off! I founded and ran a successful marketing program for military families who had loved ones in Iraq. This unique program offered free services to military families with members in Iraq for shipping, phone messages, and personal delivery of gifts for their loved ones. I also liaised with base command to ensure all regulations and policies were met.

My expertise includes:
- Entrepreneurial spirit and creativity
- Communications and liaison
- Writing and marketing strategies
- Community relations
- Caring for military families and veterans

Experience

Public Affairs Specialist

US Navy Reserves

February 2012 – Present (2 years 3 months) | Hampton, Virginia Area

Successfully landed excellent position as GS-9 Public Affairs Specialist in charge of all advertising for recruiting program.

> **Employers search LinkedIn by zip code, which is automatically tied to your city and state.**
>
> **Moving? Put your NEW location into your LinkedIn account.**

PARTNER/MANAGER

Sendmilitarycoupons.com
September 2010 – February 2011 (6 months) | San Diego, CA

MARKETING PROGRAM FOR MILITARY FAMILIES WITH FAMILY MEMBER IN IRAQ. Developed, owned, managed and operated business that sold marketing contracts to local businesses. Marketed "Send It To Your Sweetie" program targeting free services to military families with members in Iraq for shipping, phone messages, and personal delivery of gifts for their loved ones. Met with base command to ensure all regulations and policies were met.

• Accomplishment: Conceptualized a successful program for family members to send gifts and messages to military personnel. More than 2,500 messages were sent through this program in just 6 months. Sold business in less than 6 months for a substantial profit.

COMMUNICATIONS. Wrote business plan and developed all aspects of advertising and marketing. Performed cold calls on business customers and followed up with written proposals. Created and delivered PowerPoint presentations to groups of various sizes. Organized and prepared mailings to families and businesses.

WEBSITE DESIGN: Designed website and prepared spreadsheet to track monthly views and clicks. Due to volume of business, interviewed and hired 3 contractors to assist with billing, designing ads, and updating website.

MANAGER

Self-Promotions Biz Cards
June 2005 – July 2009 (4 years 2 months) | 29 Palms, CA

CREATIVE PRODUCTION: Sold and created full-color, personalized business cards to small businesses. Planned and organized work; efficiently and effectively processed the sale, design, ordering and delivery of product. Ensured quality control and timeliness for re-orders.

• Established a successful in-home business with local producers of business cards. Contracted with more than 15 vendors and tracked orders for more than 200 customers in two years. Efficiently set up and managed own schedule and schedule for automatic reordering.

CUSTOMER SERVICES: Provided administrative support to customers and vendors. Prepared and sent invoices, collected. Conducted all aspects of accounting.

COMMUNICATION: Corresponded with clients by email and phone, ensured correct grammar, spelling and format. Made cold calls on small businesses – utilized interpersonal skills to develop customer base of 300 businesses within 6 months.

COMPUTER SKILLS: Utilized typing speed of 45 wpm, Microsoft Suite programs for reports and communication, as well as Photoshop, Illustrator and Corel software to design cards.

Demonstrated strong customer services skills; multi-tasked and worked under pressure and constant deadlines. Maintained customer relations; photographed clients and worked with customers to achieve their desired customized product.

PUBLIC RELATIONS

Chiropractic Health-Care
February 2004 – January 2005 (1 year) | San Diego, CA

BUSINESS DEVELOPMENT AND COMMUNICATIONS: Represented chiropractic clinic public relations, made new business contacts, mended old contacts. Developed lasting business relationships with store managers, district managers and their assistants both inside and outside the office. Scheduled health screenings involving blood pressure, glucose and cholesterol testing. Ensured excellent service. Successfully increased patient roster by an average of 5 new patients per week.

STORE MANAGER

Lulu's Boutique

April 2002 – February 2004 (1 year 11 months) | Los Angeles, CA

ADMINISTRATION: Performed office and store administration including management of files and official records, training, payroll and reporting. Communicated effectively orally and in writing. Developed, wrote, standardized and regulated customer service procedures, policies and systems.

COMMUNICATIONS: Communicated with diverse customers, vendors, management to increase sales and resolve problems. Greeted and assisted customers with special requests. Trained staff to deliver excellent customer service.

COMPUTER SKILLS: Utilized computer skills to design website and regulate maintenance for user effectiveness. Used Microsoft Word for correspondence and Excel for reports. Ensured accuracy, correct grammar, spelling, punctuation and syntax.

MANAGED STAFF AND BUDGET: Planned and organized work for sales staff; managed budgeting for cost effective sales planning, directed all tasks and aspects of controlling, maintaining and rotating inventory. Designed store layout and product presentations.

MARKETING SOLUTIONS: Gathered pertinent data, and recognized solutions to initiate and conduct successful storewide marketing campaigns. Controlled and minimized expenses to maximize profit through selected business improvements.

 Languages

Spanish   **French**

 Skills & Endorsements

Microsoft Office

Spanish

French

Graphic Design

Education

Devry University-California

2000 – 2002

Activities and Societies: Marketing and Business Courses

STEP 3

Research Vacancy Announcements on USAJOBS

The best way to understand where you fit in government is to search for jobs that fit your experience and interests. Federal vacancy announcements (job advertisements) contain all of the information you need to compare your background to the position requirements.

Types of Federal Job Openings

When you are searching for a federal job, it is helpful to know that there are generally four types of vacancies.

Competitive Service jobs are posted on USAJOBS.

Excepted Service Agencies are not required to post jobs on USAJOBS.

Excepted Service Positions are jobs which also do not have to be posted on USAJOBS.

Find a link to the list of Excepted Service Agencies and Excepted Service Positions at www.resume-place.com/resources/useful-links/.

Agencies can also make **direct hires** for critical need positions or in situations where there is a shortage of candidates. All direct hire authority positions must be posted on USAJOBS. For a list of current direct hire authority positions, to go www.usajobs.gov and search on the keywords "direct hire."

TYPES OF FEDERAL JOBS | STEP 3

More details in the Federal Staffing Basics Quick Reference beginning on page 136.

Competitive Service Jobs

Competitive service jobs are under U.S. Office of Personnel Management's (OPM) jurisdiction and follow laws to ensure that applicants and employees receive fair and equal treatment in the hiring process. Selecting officials have broad authority to review more than one applicant source before determining the best-qualified candidate based on job-related criteria. Positions are open to the public. For positions lasting more than 120 days, vacancies must be announced and posted on USAJOBS, the federal government's central repository of job information. Veterans' preference rules are applied. Candidates are ranked and referred in order, i.e., highest scoring candidates or candidates in the highest quality group are referred first for selection. However, compensable disabled veterans "float" to the top, except for scientific and professional upper-level positions.

Excepted Service Jobs

Excepted service jobs are the jobs with agencies that set their own qualification requirements and are not subject to the appointment, pay, and classification rules in Title 5, United States Code. These agencies are able to be more flexible with recruitment incentives, salaries, promotions, and other personnel matters. They are also subject to veterans' preference. Positions may be in the excepted service by law, executive order, or action of OPM. Excepted service jobs are not required to be posted on USAJOBS. To learn about their job opportunities, you must go to the specific agency websites.

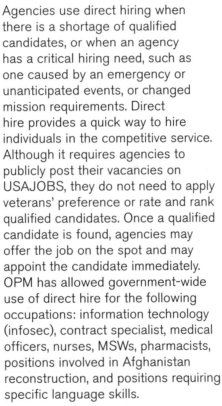

Direct Hire

Agencies use direct hiring when there is a shortage of qualified candidates, or when an agency has a critical hiring need, such as one caused by an emergency or unanticipated events, or changed mission requirements. Direct hire provides a quick way to hire individuals in the competitive service. Although it requires agencies to publicly post their vacancies on USAJOBS, they do not need to apply veterans' preference or rate and rank qualified candidates. Once a qualified candidate is found, agencies may offer the job on the spot and may appoint the candidate immediately. OPM has allowed government-wide use of direct hire for the following occupations: information technology (infosec), contract specialist, medical officers, nurses, MSWs, pharmacists, positions involved in Afghanistan reconstruction, and positions requiring specific language skills.

Pathways

Executive Order 13562, dated December 27, 2010, established a comprehensive structure to help the federal government be more competitive in recruiting and hiring talented individuals who are in school or who have recently received a degree. Student and recent graduate programs are to be consolidated into three clear program paths: internship program, recent graduate program, and the Presidential Management Fellows (PMF) program.

"Dual Status" Military Technicians

"Dual status" military technicians are federal civilian employees who are required to maintain military reserve status as a condition of their employment and are generally required to maintain membership in the National Guard as a condition of their employment. Military technicians are assigned to civilian positions in administration and training of reserve component units, or in maintaining and repairing reserve component supplies and equipment. They are required to attend weekend drills and annual training with their reserve unit, and can be involuntarily ordered to active duty the same way as other members of the Selected Reserve. The Department of Defense, the Army, the Air Force, and the National Guard Bureau all oversee dual-status technicians.

HOW TO SEARCH USAJOBS

About 5,000 job announcements are posted on USAJOBS (www.usajobs.gov) every day! Learn how to search effectively and efficiently to locate the vacancy announcements that are best for you.

Search by Keyword and Geographic Location

This is the easiest search to perform and will return a large number of results.

- Go to the USAJOBS home page.

- Enter keywords and geographic location.

- Try to use keywords specific to your unique skill set or the correct job title in quotation marks.

USAJOBS Advanced Search

You can quickly and efficiently refine your USAJOBS job announcement search using the Advanced Search function. For example:

- Search for federal jobs with certain grade or salary level in a certain geographic region
- Search for all jobs worldwide for a certain agency
- Search for all jobs within a certain occupational series or keyword either worldwide or within a certain geographic location

```
 Home    Search Jobs    My Account    Resource Center              SIGN IN OR CREATE AN ACCOUNT

USAJOBS
"WORKING FOR AMERICA"

Please enter at least one of the following in order to perform a search: Keyword, occupational series or job category, location, or agency.

Show: All Expanded  All Collapsed

▼  Keywords ?

Search for:     [ All of these words ⇕ ]    Job Title, Agency Name, Job Announcement #, etc

But none of these words:

Search by Job Title:

▶  Salary or Pay Grade ?

▶  Occupational Series or Job Category ?

▶  Location ?

▶  Department and Agency ?

▶  Type of Work or Work Schedule

▶  Posting Options ?

Who May Apply ?

Are you:
   • a current or former Federal civilian employee who holds or held a non-temporary appointment
        • In the competitive service in the Executive Branch or in a position not in the Executive branch specifically included in the competitive
          service by statute, or
        • In an excepted service position covered by an interchange agreement, or
        • Eligible for reinstatement?

   • A Veteran eligible for veterans' preference or separated from the armed forces under honorable conditions after 3 years or more of continuous military
     service?
   • A person with non-competitive appointment eligibility?

        ◉ No - I do not fall into one of these categories and only want to see jobs open to the general public.
        ○ Yes - I fall into one of these categories and want to see all jobs open to applicants with the above eligibilities, such as federal
          employees.
```

For the above question "Who May Apply":
- If you are a veteran, Schedule A, or any of the choices above, answer YES.
- If you have no special hiring program consideration, answer NO.

STEP 3 | CRITICAL VACANCY ANNOUNCEMENT FEATURES

Follow the Directions!

The following items are the most important elements of a vacancy announcement. Be sure to study these items on every announcement so that you follow the directions successfully.

 ### Closing Date – The Closing Dates are Getting Closer!

Due to the number of applications, many closing dates are getting shorter even to just 1-2 days. Get your federal resume written in advance so that you are ready to apply when you find the perfect USAJOBS announcement. If an announcement reads "Open Continuously" or "Inventory Building," or has a closing date that is 12 months away, then this announcement is a database-building announcement. Submit your application at least one day early in case there is a complication with the submission. NOTE: Disabled veterans CAN apply to positions after the closing date, but it is better to submit on time.

Who May Apply

Read this section first to see if you can apply for the position. Some announcements are open only to current employees of the hiring agency.

Duties

The description of duties will be written based on the actual position description. The write-up will include "keywords" that should be included in a federal resume.

Qualifications

Are you qualified? Read the qualifications to determine if you have the general and specialized qualifications. If the announcement states one year, that means 52 weeks, 40 hours per week.

 ### Knowledge, Skills, and Abilities are KEYWORDS!

If KSAs are listed in the announcement, you will need to cover them in the federal resume. Follow the Outline Format federal resume examples featured in this book with the KSAs for headlines in your work experience descriptions. Then add an accomplishment that will demonstrate your KSAs.

 ### How to Apply

Carefully read the "how to apply" instructions as they will differ from agency to agency.

The usual application includes a resume, KSAs (if requested separately), last performance evaluation (if possible), DD-214 (if you were in the military), and transcripts (if requested or if you are applying based on education).

 ### Questionnaires – Beware, this is a TEST! You need 85 to 90!

In the "Self-Assessment Questionnaires" you rate your own skill and experience. Do not deflate your answers. Give yourself all the credit that you can. Your Questionnaire score must be 85 to 90 in order to get Best Qualified. PLUS … Your resume must match your answers to the questions. Human Resources will compare the Questionnaire to your resume.

SPECIALIZED
EXPERIENCE

SPECIALIZED EXPERIENCE IS YOUR POT OF GOLD

The requirements for specialized experience MUST be covered in your federal resume in order to pass the first hurdle and be rated qualified for the position. This is a deal breaker! The HR specialist will be looking for the "One Year Specialized Experience" at the "next lower grade / salary level" in your resume. Learn how to match your resume to the POT of GOLD in the announcement.

Sample USAJOBS Vacancy Announcement #1

CIVILIAN CAREERS

REAL-WORLD CHALLENGES **REAL-LIFE** REWARDS

DEPARTMENT OF THE NAVY

Job Title: IT SPECIALIST (INFOSEC)
Department: Department of the Navy
Agency: Naval Sea Systems Command
Hiring Organization: Naval Surface Warfare Center Indian Head Explosive Ordnance Disposal Technology Division

SALARY RANGE:	$76,378.00 to $139,523.00 / Per Year
OPEN PERIOD:	Friday, April 10, 2015 to Wednesday, April 15, 2015
SERIES & GRADE:	NT-2210-05

QUALIFICATIONS REQUIRED:

In order to qualify for this position, your resume must provide sufficient experience and/or education, knowledge, skills, and abilities, to perform the duties of the specific position for which you are being considered. Your resume is the key means we have for evaluating your skills, knowledge, and abilities, as they relate to this position. Therefore, we encourage you to be clear and specific when describing your experience.

Your resume must demonstrate at least one year of specialized experience at or equivalent to the (NT-04 pay band (GS-11/12 equivalency) in the Federal service or equivalent experience in the private or public sector developing or maintaining secure information systems and networks for an organization. Specialized experience is defined as experience that is typically in or related to the work of the position to be filled and has equipped you with the particular knowledge, skills, and abilities, to successfully perform the duties of the position.

Examples of qualifying experience may include, but is not limited to:
• Analyzing security reviews for information systems and networks;
• Identifying and eliminating vulnerabilities to systems and networks;
• Ensuring confidentiality, integrity, and availability of information systems, network services, data, and capabilities;
• Maintaining security integration for information systems;
• Ensuring adherence to regulations in the acquisition, maintenance, operation, and disposal of required hardware, support services and other materials;

SAMPLE USAJOBS VACANCY ANNOUNCEMENT #2

KEYWORDS

KEYWORDS FOR RESUME SUCCESS

Find the keywords in the announcement (in bold below) and use them in your resume to demonstrate your qualifications for this job.

Army Installation Management Agency

Job Title: Community Recreation Officer, NF-05
Department: Department of the Army
Agency: Army Installation Management Command
Hiring Organization: USAG WIESBADEN, DFMWR, COMMUNITY RECREATION DIVISION
Job Announcement Number: EUNAFJD151368909

SALARY RANGE:	$85,000.00 to $105,000.00 / Per Year
OPEN PERIOD:	Monday, April 13, 2015 to Monday, April 27, 2015
SERIES & GRADE:	NF-0301-05
POSITION INFORMATION:	Full Time - Permanent
PROMOTION POTENTIAL:	05

DUTIES:

Through subordinate activity managers, is responsible for overall **management of fiscal resources** and direction of the Directorate, Morale Welfare and Recreation (DMWR) **Community Recreation** Division at a large garrison, to include most of the following programs: **Sports, Fitness and Aquatics**, Extramural Sports Region Championships, Auto Skills, Parks and Picnic Areas, Library, Entertainment, Music and Theater, Arts and Crafts, Community Activity Centers, Outdoor Recreation, Leisure Travel, Better Opportunities for Single Soldiers (BOSS), and non-facility based programs. **Provides leadership and supervision**, and communicates mission and organization goals to subordinates.

Provides policies and guidance to ensure attainment of the established objectives of the division. Directs, develops, and **administers plans and procedures; implements regulations** to provide for a comprehensive community recreation program widely recognized for addressing a **broad range of interests and needs** of the military community. **Institutes innovative programs** to meet future needs, including development and support of **contingency operations** for mobilization and demobilization. **Coordinates and markets program** within the community. **Develops policy and strategic plans** addressing resources, facilities, and programs.

Reviews program priorities and develops five-year plan covering projected programs of personnel, funds, and facilities. Serves as the **Garrison representative and advisor** on matters relating to recreation and morale support of soldiers and their Families.

QUALIFICATIONS REQUIRED:

Work experience directing/managing one or more DMWR Recreation Programs for a garrison, or similar civilian operation, for at least one year.

Conditions of employment:
1. A one-year probationary period may be required.
2. Meet all qualification/eligibility requirements.
3. Satisfactorily complete an employment verification check.
4. Successfully complete all required background checks.
5. A completed and signed copy DA Form 3433-1 is required prior to entrance on duty.
6. Incumbent is required to submit a Financial Disclosure Statement, OGE-450, Executive Branch Personnel Confidential Financial Disclosure Report upon entering the position and annually, in accordance with DoD Directive 5500-7-R, Joint Ethics Regulation, dated 30 August 1993.
7. Incumbent must file a Confidential Statement of Affiliations and Financial Interest in accordance with the requirements of AR 600-50.

HOW YOU WILL BE EVALUATED:

Applicants who posses the following will be considered as best qualified

1. Experience with RECTRAC or other **automated inventory systems**.
2. Experience with **budgeting and internal controls**?
3. Experience **briefing** senior leadership or civilian equivalent?
4. Experience with **planning and executing large scale events**?
5. Experience with **Installation Status Reports (ISR)** or civilian programs that evaluates facilities infrastructure according to prescribed standards to determine its readiness to meet current and future missions?
6. Experience with Common Levels of Support (CLS) or a civilian equivalent matrix system that **measures operational performance**, effectiveness, and customer satisfaction?

Applicants meeting both minimum qualifications and best qualified criteria will be referred to the selection manager prior to those who meet only the minimum qualifications.**

SAMPLE USAJOBS VACANCY ANNOUNCEMENT #3

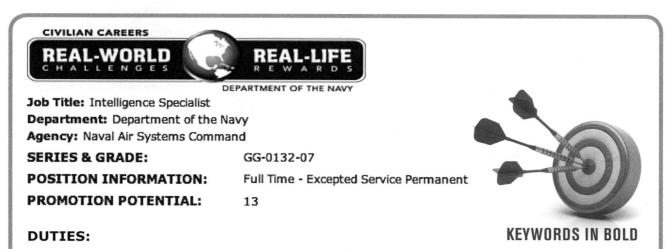

CIVILIAN CAREERS

REAL-WORLD CHALLENGES **REAL-LIFE** REWARDS

DEPARTMENT OF THE NAVY

Job Title: Intelligence Specialist
Department: Department of the Navy
Agency: Naval Air Systems Command

SERIES & GRADE: GG-0132-07

POSITION INFORMATION: Full Time - Excepted Service Permanent

PROMOTION POTENTIAL: 13

KEYWORDS IN BOLD

DUTIES:

- Employee performs **basic research and analysis** utilizing **all-source intelligence, databases, assessments, and/or products in support of assigned programs** within the Naval Aviation Enterprise (NAE), with a primary focus on intelligence support for Mission, Engineering, and Analysis; PEO Unmanned Aerial Vehicles and Cyber Threats.

- Participate in the **research, formulation, and presentation of oral briefings** and **written products for assigned customers** under the guidance of a senior analyst.

- The analyst will utilize **JWICS, to conduct research, communicate** with other analysts and subject matter experts, and utilize external **intelligence databases**.

QUALIFICATIONS REQUIRED:

In order to qualify for this position, your resume must provide sufficient experience and/or education, knowledge, skills, and abilities, to perform the duties of the specific position. Your resume is the key means we have for evaluating your skills, knowledge, and abilities, as they relate to this position. Therefore, we encourage you to be clear and specific when describing your experience.

SPECIALIZED EXPERIENCE

Your resume must demonstrate at least one year of specialized experience at or equivalent to the GG/GS-07 grade level or pay band in the Federal service equivalent experience in the private or public sector. Specialized experience is defined as experience that is typically in or related to the work of the position to be filled and has equipped you with the particular knowledge, skills, and abilities to successfully perform the duties of the position. Specialized experience must demonstrate the following: **1) Research specific intelligence information in preparation of studies; 2) Extract all significant data pertaining to cyber-based intrusions; 3) Assist senior analysts with providing intelligence products.**

HOW YOU WILL BE EVALUATED:

When the application process is complete, we will review your resume to ensure you meet the hiring eligibility and qualification requirements listed in this announcement. You will be rated based on the information provided in your resume and responses to the questionnaire, along with your supporting documentation to determine your ability to demonstrate the following knowledge, skills and abilities/competencies:
- **RESEARCH**
- **INTELLIGENCE ANALYSIS**
- **INTELLIGENCE DATABASES**

Give yourself all the credit that you can when selecting your answers. There are multiple ways to give an E answer. Make sure your answers are supported in your resume!

Questionnaire: Intelligence Specialist

For your information, below is an example of the rating scale that applicants will use to answer competency based assessment questions.

A- I do not have experience or demonstrated capability in performing this activity, but I am willing to learn.

B- I have limited experience in performing this activity. I have had exposure to this activity but would require additional guidance, instruction, or experience to perform it at a satisfactory level.

C- I have a fair amount of experience and a fair amount of demonstrated capability in performing this activity. I can perform this activity satisfactorily but could benefit from additional guidance, instruction, or experience to perform this activity more effectively.

D- I have considerable experience and capability in performing this task. I can perform this task independently and effectively.

E- I have extensive experience in performing this task. I am considered an expert; I am able to train or assist others; and my work is typically not reviewed by a supervisor. I have received verbal and/or written recognition from other in carrying out this task.

2. Perform basic **research and analysis** utilizing all source intelligence.

3. Research and assist in the preparation of **briefings and written products** for assigned customers.

4. **Conduct research; communicate** with other analysts and subject matter experts utilizing external **intelligence databases**.

5. Utilize **intelligence regulations and directives** to include intelligence oversight as well as applicable security procedures and policies of collateral and sensitive compartmental information.

KEYWORDS IN BOLD

6. Participate with higher grade analysts in **researching for specific intelligence information** in preparation of routine **studies** or portions of complex studies.

As previously explained, your responses in this Assessment Questionnaire are subject to evaluation and verification. Later steps in the selection process are specifically designed to verify your responses. Deliberate attempts to falsify information will be grounds for disqualifying you or for dismissing you from employment following acceptance. Please take this opportunity to review your responses to ensure their accuracy.

STEP 4

Analyze Your Core Competencies

Besides specialized experience, education, and technical skills, what "value-added" competencies can you offer a supervisor?

What are competencies?

OPM defines a competency as a measurable pattern of knowledge, skills, abilities, behaviors, and other characteristics that an individual needs to perform work roles or occupational functions successfully. Successful job performance requires a broad range of competencies, such as technical knowledge, analytical abilities, and interpersonal skills. "Competencies can be seen as <u>basic qualities that employees should exhibit in the work place to maximize their potential for the government</u>."

Core Competencies Are Your Transferable Skills!

If you are changing your career, these core competencies will demonstrate that you have valuable skills that are transferable to your new career.

How Do I Use Core Competencies When Applying for Jobs?

These characteristics go above and beyond skills. You can stand out in a government resume, question/essay narrative, or behavior-based interview by highlighting these competencies. Study this step and determine the top five or ten competencies that make you a stand-out employee in your field of work. Add these competencies to your resume in the work experience descriptions for a stronger federal resume!

See resume samples on pages 80, 88, and 94 for transferable skills / core competencies in a federal resume.

Office of Personnel Management (OPM) Competencies

Find your core competencies and check them off the list. Add a few of these competencies into the "duties" section of your work experience.

Interpersonal Effectiveness

❑ Builds and sustains positive relationships.

❑ Handles conflicts and negotiations effectively.

❑ Builds and sustains trust and respect.

❑ Collaborates and works well with others.

❑ Shows sensitivity and compassion for others.

❑ Encourages shared decision-making.

❑ Recognizes and uses ideas of others.

❑ Communicates clearly, both orally and in writing.

❑ Listens actively to others.

❑ Honors commitments and promises.

Customer Service

❑ Understands that customer service is essential to achieving our mission.

❑ Understands and meets the needs of internal customers.

❑ Manages customer complaints and concerns effectively and promptly.

❑ Designs work processes and systems that are responsive to customers.

❑ Ensures that daily work and the strategic direction are customer-centered.

❑ Uses customer feedback data in planning and providing products and services.

❑ Encourages and empowers subordinates to meet or exceed customer needs and expectations.

❑ Identifies and rewards behaviors that enhance customer satisfaction.

Flexibility/Adaptability

❑ Responds appropriately to new or changing situations.

❑ Handles multiple inputs and tasks simultaneously.

❑ Seeks and welcomes the ideas of others.

❑ Works well with all levels and types of people.

❑ Accommodates new situations and realities.

❑ Remains calm in high-pressure situations.

❑ Makes the most of limited resources.

❑ Demonstrates resilience in the face of setbacks.

❑ Understands change management.

OPM Competencies cont.

Creative Thinking

❑ Appreciates new ideas and approaches.

❑ Thinks and acts innovatively.

❑ Looks beyond current reality and the "status quo".

❑ Demonstrates willingness to take risks.

❑ Challenges assumptions.

❑ Solves problems creatively.

❑ Demonstrates resourcefulness.

❑ Fosters creative thinking in others.

❑ Allows and encourages employees to take risks.

❑ Identifies opportunities for new projects and acts on them.

❑ Rewards risk-taking and non-successes and values what was learned.

Systems Thinking

❑ Understands the complexities of the agency and how the "product" is delivered.

❑ Appreciates the consequences of specific actions on other parts of the system.

❑ Thinks in context.

❑ Knows how one's role relates to others in the organization.

❑ Demonstrates awareness of the purpose, process, procedures, and outcomes of one's work.

❑ Encourages and rewards collaboration.

Organizational Stewardship

❑ Demonstrates commitment to people.

❑ Empowers and trusts others.

❑ Develops leadership skills and opportunities throughout organization.

❑ Develops team-based improvement processes.

❑ Promotes future-oriented system change.

❑ Supports and encourages lifelong learning throughout the organization.

❑ Manages physical, fiscal, and human resources to increase the value of products and services.

❑ Builds links between individuals and groups in the organization.

❑ Integrates organization into the community.

❑ Accepts accountability for self, others, and the organization's development.

❑ Works to accomplish the organizational business plan.

Transportation Security Administration Core Competencies

The Transportation Security Administration (TSA) has posted its catalog of competencies containing both core and technical competencies at **www.tsa.gov/assets/pdf/competencies_and_definitions.pdf**. Below is a sampling of core competency definitions from the catalog.

Accountability	Holds self and others accountable for measurable high-quality, timely, and cost-effective results; determines objectives, sets priorities and delegates work; accepts responsibility for mistakes; complies with established control systems and rules.
Administration and Management	Applies business and management principles involved in strategic planning, resource allocation, and coordination of people and resources in support of organizational operations.
Administrative Procedures and Tasks	Performs administrative responsibilities following guidelines and procedures; provides guidance to others; coordinates services, researches problems, and recommends changes.
Arithmetic and Mathematical Reasoning	Performs computations such as addition, subtraction, multiplication, and division correctly; solves practical problems by choosing appropriately from a variety of mathematical techniques such as formulas and percentages.
Attention to Detail	Is thorough and precise when accomplishing a task with concern for all aspects of the job involved; double-checks the accuracy of information and work products to provide consistently accurate and high-quality work.
Coaching & Mentoring	Provides clear, behaviorally specific performance feedback; makes suggestions for improvement in a manner that builds confidence and preserves self-esteem; works with individuals to develop improvement plans and achieve performance goals.
Command Presence	Demonstrates confidence, credibility, and professionalism in presence, demeanor, and conduct in performance of duties within the work environment.
Conflict Management	Encourages creative tension and differences of opinions; anticipates and takes steps to prevent counter-productive confrontations; manages and resolves conflicts and disagreements in a constructive manner.
Conscientiousness	Demonstrates responsible and dependable behavior; takes responsibility for personal performance through a high level of effort and commitment.

Department of Homeland Security (DHS) Competencies

The DHS competencies are comparable with those for DOD, IC, and OPM, including the following communication skills:

- Report writing
- Verbal/speech
- Problem solving / Decision-making

The other competencies for DHS are focused on overall requirements for the Department.

OPM Competencies

The OPM competencies related to the DOD requirements in the following areas:

- Interpersonal skills
- Teamwork, learning
- Decision making
- Customer service
- Accountability

DOD Competencies

As listed in the DOD Competencies and compared with the DHS, OPM, and IC, the most important/reoccurring requirements were the following:

- Interpersonal skills
- Integrity
- Written and oral communication
- Continual learning
- Strategic thinking
- Team building
- Accountability
- Decisiveness
- Customer service
- Problem solving
- Technical credibility
- Enterprise-wide perspective

From https://nstii.com/content/core-competencies

SENIOR EXECUTIVE SERVICE CORE COMPETENCIES | STEP 4

Office of Personnel Management, Senior Executive Service, Executive Core Qualifications (ECQs)

Leading Change	Leading People	Results Driven	Business Acumen	Building Coalitions
Definitions				
This core qualification involves the ability to bring about strategic change, both within and outside the organization, to meet organizational goals. Inherent to this ECQ is the ability to establish an organizational vision and to implement it in a continuously changing environment.	This core qualification involves the ability to lead people toward meeting the organization's vision, mission, and goals. Inherent to this ECQ is the ability to provide an inclusive workplace that fosters the development of others, facilitates cooperation and teamwork, and supports constructive resolution of conflicts.	This core qualification involves the ability to meet organizational goals and customer expectations. Inherent to this ECQ is the ability to make decisions that produce high-quality results by applying technical knowledge, analyzing problems, and calculating risks.	This core qualification involves the ability to manage human, financial, and information resources strategically.	This core qualification involves the ability to build coalitions internally and with other federal agencies, state and local governments, nonprofit and private sector organizations, foreign governments, or international organizations to achieve common goals.
Competencies				
Creativity and Innovation External Awareness Flexibility Resilience Strategic Thinking Vision	Conflict Management Leveraging Diversity Developing Others Team Building	Accountability Customer Service Decisiveness Entrepreneurship Problem Solving Technical Credibility	Financial Management Human Capital Management Technology Management	Partnering Political Savvy Influencing/ Negotiating

More Information and Samples: *The New SES Application*, D. Hudson and K. Troutman

STEP 5

Analyze Vacancy Announcements for Keywords

Adding keywords is important for both a federal resume and a private industry resume. Your goal is to match your resume as closely as possible to your target announcement and demonstrate that you DO have the experience for their position.

Where Do I Find Keywords?

- **Vacancy Announcements**: Focus your search in these sections: Duties, Specialized Experience, Qualifications, and the Assessment Questionnaire.

- **Agency or Organizational Mission:** You may find this in the vacancy announcement or on the agency's website.

- **Core Competencies**: See Step 4 for more information about core competencies.

- **Occupational Standards**: It's not widely known yet that occupational standards are superb sources for keywords to use in your resume!

O*Net OnLine

Find keywords for all jobs!
www.onetonline.org

HOW DO I FIND KEYWORDS? |

KEYWORDS

Steps to Finding Keywords in a Vacancy Announcement

1. Find ONE GOOD target vacancy announcement.

2. You will be reviewing these sections from the announcement for keywords:

   ✪ Duties

   ✪ Qualifications

   ✪ Specialized Experience

   ✪ Questionnaires

   ✪ Agency or organization mission

3. Copy and paste these sections from the announcement into a word processing program such as MS Word.

4. Enlarge the type to 14 or 16 points to make the print more readable.

5. Separate each sentence by increasing the line spacing for the entire document.

6. Delete useless words such as "the incumbent will" or "duties will encompass a variety of tasks including."

7. Underline or highlight keywords and skills that are significant to the position, such as "identifying deficiencies in human performance" and "recommending changes for correction."

How Many Keywords Do I Need?

At a minimum, include at least five to seven keywords and keyword phrases in your resume. However, the more keywords you can include to help translate your experience into terms that the Human Resources specialist can clearly identify, the greater your chances of having the HR specialist understand how your qualifications match the desired qualifications in the vacancy announcement.

Now MATCH Your Resume to the Keywords

Once you have drafted a basic resume, you MUST MATCH this resume to these keywords. Don't try to use the same resume to apply for a number of different vacancy announcements. The ALL CAP WORDS in an Outline Format resume are phrases and keywords from the announcements. (See more on this in Step 6.) The Human Resources specialist and supervisor will recognize these skills from their announcement.

EXAMPLES OF KEYWORDS

In the examples on the following pages, the found keywords are identified in bold type as well as listed at the end of each example.

Keywords can be found in the Duties and Qualifications sections of a vacancy announcement.

1702 Child and Youth Program Assistant (Entry Level, CY-01) Department of the Army / Army Installation Management Command

DUTIES:

Serves as a **Child and Youth Program Assistant** (CYPA) in one or more CYS programs. Maintains control of and accounts for whereabouts and safety of children and youth. Assists in providing and **leading planned activities** for program participants.

Helps establish a program environment that promotes **positive child and youth interactions** with other children, youth and adults. Helps prepare, arrange, and **maintain indoor and outdoor activity** areas and materials to accommodate daily schedule. Uses **prepared curriculum/program** materials and assists with developing a list of needed supplies and equipment.

Interacts with children and youth using approved **child guidance and youth development techniques**. Interacts professionally with staff members, parents, and the Command.

Supervises children and youth during daily schedule of indoor and outdoor activities, on field trips, outings and special events. Promotes and models safety, fitness, health and nutrition practices. Notifies supervisor on health, fire, and safety compliance concerns.

Observes a program participant for signs that may indicate illness, abuse or neglect and reports as directed. Notes special instructions provided by parents.

KEYWORDS

Child and Youth Program Assistant

Lead planned activities

Promote positive child and youth interactions

Maintain indoor and outdoor activities

Prepare curriculum and program materials

Utilize child guidance and youth development techniques

Supervise children and youth with indoor and outdoor activities

Observe program participants

7401 Food and Beverage Attendant, Army Installation Management Agency

DUTIES:
Performs all of the following duties on a recurring basis:
Collects sales slips, total sales on **cash register,** accepts payment from patrons and makes change as necessary. Maintains related cash records. Keeps **work area clean and orderly.**

Sets up **food service counters** and steam tables with hot and cold foods and beverages. Prepares coffee and hot water for tea, fills beverage dispensers with juices and soft drinks.

Sets tables, seats guests, records guests' selections and turns in orders to the kitchen. Serves food, alcoholic and nonalcoholic beverages. Presents bill and receives payment. Cleans tables and immediate area.

Prepares fruits and vegetables for cooking and serving. Makes a variety of fruit and vegetable salads. Portions out food, cleans and prepares meats and seafood for cooking. Checks food during cooking to prevent overcooking. Unloads trucks and places contents in proper storage and use areas, brings supplies to work areas. Clean floors, walls and windows in kitchen, dining and storage areas.

Skill and Knowledge: **Able to work alone.** Know the proper use of special cleaning and sanitizing solutions. Know **simple food handling techniques. Able to work safely.** Able to serve uniform individual portions and avoid distractions when several guests ask for different items at the same time. Able to use simple arithmetic.

KEYWORDS

Utilize cash register and collect payments

Food handling

Safety procedures

Prepare fruits and vegetables for cooking and serving

Setting tables, seating guests, and customer services

EXAMPLES OF KEYWORDS CONT.

Keywords can be found in the OPM Classification Standards.

0341   Administrative Officer

CLASSIFICATION STANDARD

An administrative officer is a generalist. The total management process is his interest, and the proficiency required involves many aspects of management. **General management skills** are the paramount requirement. Though aspects such as **budget administration and personnel management** assume major importance in many positions and other aspects such as procurement and property management are also important in many jobs, no single functional, resource or service area forms a basis for the paramount skills.

Administrative officer positions typically include such duties and responsibilities as the following, or comparable duties:

1. Helping management to **identify its financial, personnel, and material needs and problems.**

2. **Developing budget estimates** and justifications; making sure that funds are used in accordance with the operating budget.

3. **Counseling management** in developing and maintaining sound organization structures, improving management methods and procedures, and seeing to the effective use of men, money, and materials.

4. **Collaborating** with personnel specialists in **finding solutions** to management problems arising out of changes in work which have an impact on jobs and employees.

5. **Advising on and negotiating contracts**, agreements, and cooperative arrangements with other government agencies, universities, or private organizations.

Administrative officer positions are mainly of two broad types. One type is the chief of a central administrative unit which provides services to a number of operating divisions, field offices, or other units each headed by an operating manager. The central administrative unit includes specialist positions in various areas such as **budget, data processing,** etc. The administrative unit chief has considerable authority to complete **personnel actions, obligate funds, make purchases,** etc.

KEYWORDS

Management advisor

Supervisor

Budget advisor

Problem-solving of management problems

Advise on and negotiate contracts

Data analyst

Keywords can be found in the KSAs and Quality Ranking Factors in Announcements.

0343 Management/ Program Analyst

DUTIES:

In this position, you will strengthen the Department's ability to perform homeland security functions by **developing policies,** conducting **special studies,** and providing **technical assistance.** Typical work assignments include:

- **Developing and evaluating policies** in assigned program areas such as reviewing **existing strategic and workforce management plans** and proposing potential changes to ensure plans represent organizational priorities and ensuring that comprehensive succession management planning is in place.
- **Analyzing existing management techniques**, processes, and plans for improving organizational effectiveness.
- **Evaluating policies and recommending actions** to achieve organizational objectives such as analyzing organizational programs and processes to determine whether current procedures efficiently accomplish objectives and provide sufficient controls necessary for sound management.

Quality Ranking Factor: Applicants who possess the following experience may be rated higher than applicants who do not possess this experience. The desired experience for this position includes work in **strategic planning, succession management, workforce planning and data analysis of human resource information.** Management desires experience in applying **data analysis, metrics and performance measure analysis** to **workforce planning and the development**, execution and improvement of organizational effectiveness planning.

KEYWORDS

Conduct special studies

Technical assistance on projects

Develop policies for strategic planning and workforce planning

Data analysis and performance measure analysis

Workforce planning and development

Keywords can be found in the Specialized Experience section.

Housing Manager, U.S. Marine Corps, GS-1173-09

DUTIES:
Coordinate housing projects by maintaining liaison with command officials.
Implement procedures for housing assignment and eligibility by assigning quarters ensuring integrity.
Implement a command centralized billeting inspection program by inspecting the operation of each billeting facility.
Perform inspections to ensure work is accomplished and that work requests are reconciled.
Maintain sufficient casual quarters to meet billeting needs throughout fluctuating billeting space.

QUALIFICATIONS REQUIRED:
Your resume must demonstrate **at least one year of specialized experience at or equivalent to the GS-07** grade level or pay band in the Federal service or equivalent experience in the private or public sector. Specialized experience must demonstrate the following: **Managing the operation and utilization of housing facilities, implementing procedures for housing assignment, and maintaining quarters by performing inspections**.

KEYWORDS

Manage the operation and utilization of housing facilities

Implement procedures for housing assignment

Maintain quarters by performing inspections

Meet billeting needs

Liaison with command officials and customer services

KEYWORDS

Keywords can be found in the Questionnaires.

General Supply Specialist, GS-2001

For each task in the following group, choose the statement from the list below that best describes your experience and/or training. Darken the oval corresponding to that statement in Section 25 of the Qualifications and Availability Form C. Please select only one letter for each item.

A- I have not had education, training or experience in performing this task.

B- I have had education or training in performing the task, but have not yet performed it on the job.

C- I have performed this task on the job. My work on this task was monitored closely by a supervisor or senior employee to ensure compliance with proper procedures.

D- I have performed this task as a regular part of a job. I have performed it independently and normally without review by a supervisor or senior employee.

E- I am considered an expert in performing this task. I have supervised performance of this task or am normally the person who is consulted by other workers to assist them in doing this task because of my expertise.

4. **Interpret supply management regulations**, laws, concepts, principles to determine inventory management requirements.

5. **Use automated systems** to maintain records of supply items in inventory.

6. **Establish and implement policies**, procedural guidance and instruction for personal property control.

7. Recommend and **implement supply management policies** and procedures to **ensure operational accountability of property**.

KEYWORDS

Interpret supply management regulations

Utilize supply automated systems

Implement personal property control policies

Ensure operational accountability of property

And finally, keywords can be found in organizational mission statements!

This often-overlooked resource can yield some surprisingly useful keywords. Find the mission statement for the agency or organization online and see if you can locate a few more important keywords for your resume.

STEP 6

Write Your Outline Format and Paper Federal Resumes

The OUTLINE FORMAT FEDERAL RESUME is preferred by Human Resources specialists because it is easy to read and includes keywords and accomplishments. The information that the HR specialist is looking for stands out much better in an Outline Format resume.

Here are some of the key features:

- Small paragraphs are used for readability.

- ALL CAPS keywords match keywords in the announcement.

- Accomplishments are included in the resume.

- This format copies and pastes quickly and easily into USAJOBS.

The federal resume is a reverse chronological resume.

Private Industry and TAP GPS Resume	Federal Resume
Typically 1-2 pages	**3-5 pages based on specific character lengths (use full character lengths if possible)**
Creative use of bold, underline, and other graphics	Reverse chronological resume. Traditional format with no graphics. Use CAPS for the USAJOBS Builder Resume.
No federal elements required (i.e., SSN, supervisor's name and phone, salary, veterans' preference, etc.)	Required: compliance details for each position for the last 10 years (i.e. month and years; street address, zip code, city, state, zip, country; supervisor's name; salary / GS level / military rank)
Short accomplishment bullets focused on results	Accomplishments are critical, so your resume will stand out and help you get Best Qualified
Branded "headline"	KSAs must be covered in the resume to demonstrate your specialized experience
Keywords are important	Keywords are imperative
Focus on accomplishments; less detail for position descriptions	Use blend of accomplishments and duties description with details
Profit motivated, product oriented, select customer base	Fiscal responsibility and grants, budgets, cost control, implementation of programs, legislation, serving the American public

Additional Special Considerations for Military

Military	Federal Resume
List dates of Reserve service and active duty service	**Include approx. average hours for Reserve service,** i.e., 20 years of Reserve service with deployments, equals six years of full-time work at 52 weeks per year
Include applicable awards and indicate justification for attaining award	List most awards and honors and include justification
Translate military acronyms and jargon	Translate most military acronyms and jargon, but use acronyms if the vacancy announcement uses the acronyms (i.e., DOD, DON, USMC, etc.)
Quantify and qualify military activities or acronyms	Quantify and qualify military activities or acronyms
Only include military schools/education related to the announcement	Include military service schools; indicate resident classes and total hours

Federal Resume Format

Don't use the bullet format for your resume. Is your resume a laundry list of bullets that are unrelated and not targeted to a job announcement or job series? This format will not help the Human Resources specialists to determine your qualifications for the vacancy announcement.

Use the "Outline Format" federal resume style. This format features small paragraphs, ALL CAP KEYWORDS as headlines, and a few accomplishments.

Avoid the old-school big block format. This format was popular for the Resumix keyword scanning system that was eliminated in 2010. Now, actual humans look at your resume, and large blocks of text are difficult to read.

A federal resume should be 3 to 5 pages in length. A 1 to 2-page resume does not have enough details about your experience to determine your qualifications. Resumes longer than five pages give too much information for the HR specialist to find your skills and abilities.

You MUST include the compliance information required by the Office of Personnel Management (OPM): Month and year and hours per week; employer's street address, city, state, zip code; supervisor phone number; yes/no on whether supervisor may be contacted.

Writing Style

A profile or "summary of skills" does NOT increase your application score. Your work experience must be anchored to dates, and all verbiage should be tailored to your target job. Do not include a list of generic skills.

Use active, not passive, voice. Avoid phrases such as: responsible for, duties include, assisted with, performed, provide, helped with, tasked with, recruited for, participated in, in addition to? Passive verbs create wordiness and show hiring officials that you are a merely a helper at work.

Take out as many acronyms and technical jargon as possible and replace with plain English. Make sure that anyone outside of your line of work can understand your resume, even if the hiring officials are in your field.

Use "I" very minimally in your resume.

Work Experience

Make sure that you're actually qualified for the job. Read your target job announcement from beginning to end. Contact the hiring manager listed in the announcement if you're not sure.

Match your work experience section to the target position by using keywords from the announcement. Your must use the language from the target job announcement to write your duties, responsibilities, and accomplishments.

Include your best accomplishments in the work experience section. Hiring officials want to read about your unique contributions to your job. Demonstrate that you are a star performer and not just an average one.

Federal HR only wants to see recent and relevant experience. Remove job blocks older than 20 years (for higher grade employees) and 10 years (for lower grade employees).

Include your Guard or Reserves experience and deployment details.

Education and Training

Education should be in reverse chronological order. Your current or most recent education should be at the beginning of your job block.

Expand your education section beyond just the degree and the college name. Add a list of courses and/or descriptions of three significant projects.

For training, include classroom hours and the certification title. Remove trainings that you took more than 10 years ago.

More samples and details: *Student's Federal Career Guide, 3rd Ed.*, K. Troutman and P. Binkley.

Career change federal resumes must feature relevant skills and experience for your new career.

Career Change

If you are changing your career, your resume must match the job you are targeting, not your prior career. Feature the skills that are transferable and relevant to your target job.

If you are seeking a promotion, your resume must increase in complexity to target an advanced level of performance. The resume must feature the highest, most complex level of duties, as well as your best accomplishments to demonstrate that you are ready to move up and get promoted.

How to Start Writing

Collect all of your documents and information: resumes, evaluations, position descriptions, list of training classes, college transcripts, DD-214 and other veteran's documents, etc.

Start writing your first draft using the **Classification Standards** for your target job series.

Use the Outline Format federal resume with ALL CAPS keyword headers.

Later you can tailor this draft to specific vacancy announcements.

Employment contract

BEFORE RESUME: BULLET FORMAT

Mariano separated as a 20% disabled veteran (CP), USMC Helicopter Crew. He attended college on the GI Bill, got a BS in Philosophy, and couldn't find a job. He landed a temporary federal job with the Courts Agency and finally landed a great permanent fed job with DHS.

MARIANO TORY

1234 Hillside Road Leesburg, VA 20176
(703) xxx-xxxx
mariano.tory@email.com

EXPERIENCE

United States Army (USA)
Task Force Comanche, Afghanistan, Operation Enduring Freedom   July 2010 – July 2011

- *Hazardous Materials Certifier* - Certified critical shipping documentation; marked, labeled, packed, and placarded hazardous materials for aerial, vessel, or land shipment as sole certifier of organization; and controlled compatibility of hazardous items transported and security requirements with special attention to U.S. and international laws and regulations
- *Supervisor* - Counseled, trained, and mentored personnel on subject matter performance and event-orientations, special tools utilization, equipment distribution, and accountability; serviced, maintained, and accounted for assigned equipment; and provided support to Command on pre-deployment, deployment, and re-deployment accountability of personnel, equipment, and hazardous materials
- *Tool Room Custodian* - Responsible for property accountability for the Task Force tool room; conducted monthly and quarterly inventories; and provided status reports to the company Commander
- *Tools, Measurement, Diagnostics & Equipment (TMDE) Coordinator* – Monitored projected and delinquent calibration items list; liaised on-site and off-site management of calibrated items; and briefed Task Force Executive Officer
- *Aviation Ground Support Equipment (AGSE) Technician* - Served as the Aviation Ground Support Equipment (AGSE) noncommissioned officer in charge (NCOIC); supervised compliance of AGSE accountability and distribution standards for U.S. Army company; coordinated and filed AGSE inspections, calibrations, repair and maintenance with on and off-site contractors; supported installation fire department with AGSE; and communicated AGSE status reports to Task Force Executive Officer

4th Combat Aviation Brigade, Fort Hood, Texas   July 2009 – October 2011

- *UH-60 Helicopter Maintainer* - Serviced and lubricated aircraft and subsystems and prepared aircraft for inspections and maintenance checks. Conduct scheduled inspections and assists in special inspections. Performed limited maintenance operational checks and assisted in diagnosing and troubleshooting aircraft subsystems using special tools and equipment as required. Used and performed operator maintenance on tools, special tools, and aircraft ground support equipment. Prepared forms and records related to aircraft maintenance.
- *Supervisor* - Counseled, trained, and mentored personnel on subject matter performance and event-orientations, special tools utilization, equipment distribution, and accountability; serviced, maintained, and accounted for assigned equipment; and provided support to Command on pre-deployment, deployment, and re-deployment accountability of personnel and equipment.
- *Tool Room Custodian* - Responsible for property accountability for the Task Force tool room; conducted monthly and quarterly inventories; and provided status reports to the company Commander
- *Aviation Ground Support Equipment (AGSE) Technician* - Served as the Aviation Ground Support Equipment (AGSE) non-commissioned officer in charge (NCOIC); supervised compliance of AGSE accountability and distribution standards for U.S. Army company; coordinated and filed AGSE inspections, calibrations, repair and maintenance with on-post contractors.

2nd Combat Aviation Brigade, US Army Garrison Humphreys, South Korea   July 2006 – July 2009

- *Supervisor* - Counseled, trained, and mentored personnel on subject matter performance, military education, and event-orientations
- *UH-60 Helicopter Medical Evacuation Crewmember/Maintainer* - Inspected and maintained 12 UH-60 Helicopters for aero-medical company in South Korea; provided aero-medical evacuation assistance to flight medic; visual guidance to pilots during training missions and real-life evacuation missions; and trained incoming personnel on maintenance, inspection, and flight procedures. Completed 24 real-world medevac missions and received early promotion from Private 1st Class (E-3) to Specialist (E-4)
- *UH-60 Helicopter Maintainer* - Serviced and lubricated aircraft and subsystems and ensured aircraft met inspection and maintenance compliance; performed scheduled inspections and assisted in special inspections, conducted limited maintenance operational checks, diagnosed, and troubleshot aircraft subsystems using special tools and equipment as required; conducted maintenance on tools, special tools, and aircraft ground support equipment and drafted forms and records related to aircraft maintenance.
- *Non-Combatant Evacuation Operations (NEO) Warden* - Participated in Non-Combatant Evacuation Operations (NEO) training exercises for South Korean peninsula; researched documented members' compliance with NEO standards and equipment accountability, and inspected NEO equipment prior to distribution to ensure reliable operations

SKILL SETS

- Spanish (Native or bilingual proficiency), Internet Research, Microsoft Word, PowerPoint, and Outlook, Filing, Editing, Planning, Prioritizing, Proofreading, Scheduling, Teamwork, Transcription, Scheduling, Briefing, Correspondence, Safety, Training, Liaising, Transformational and Ethical Leadership

AWARDS AND ACHIEVEMENTS

United States Army   September 2006 – November 2011

- Army Commendation Medals, Army Achievement Medals, Army Good Conduct Medal, National Defense Service Medal, Korean Defense Service Medal, Afghanistan Campaign Medal (with Service Star), Global War on Terrorism Service Medal, Non-Commissioned Officer Professional Development Ribbon, Army Service Ribbon, Overseas Service Ribbon, NATO Medal, Certificates of Achievement, Aviation Badge; Recommended for promotions (2007, 2008, and 2011), Sikorsky Aircraft Rescue Award

EDUCATION

American Military University   November 2011 – Present

- Bachelor of Arts, Philosophy (Projected to graduate May 2014)
- Concentration in Ethics

AFFILIATIONS

National Society of Collegiate Scholars, VP of Community Services   August 2013 – Present

- Establish and maintain a relationships with local service partners
- Recruit members to participate in service programs and events
- Ensure program compliance with all legal and privacy regulations

Member of: *Student Veterans of America (c.2013), Scroll and Sabre History Club (c.2013), American Philosophical Association (c.2013), Golden Key International Honours Society (c.2013), and 2nd Infantry Division Association (c.2008)*

AFTER RESUME: OUTLINE FORMAT / USAJOBS BUILDER

MARIANO TORY
1234 Hillside Road
Leesburg, VA 20176
(703) xxx-xxxx
mariano.tory@email.com

Work Experience:

S&E Bridge and Scaffold
700 Commercial Ave
Carlstadt, NJ   07072 United States

09/2014 - 12/2014
Salary: 35,000.00 USD Per Year
Hours per week: 50
Logistics and Procurement Specialist
Duties, Accomplishments and Related Skills:

ADMINISTRATIVE & CONTRACT SUPPORT. Support the Director of Operations with contract award and administration for scaffolding, hoisting, and shoring projects. Review and coordinate with other departments and companies to ensure availability of equipment or procurement items. Review and implement procurement requests for the successful completion of contracts. Oversee requisitions and timeliness to increased productivity on project sites. Create and maintain records, memoranda, evaluations, forms, and spreadsheets.

PROJECT COORDINATION. Track and monitor the progress of contracts and purchase orders. Respond to requests for information and confirm system lead times, delivery dates, and costs. Plan and implement improvements to internal and external logistical systems and processes via problem solving. Analyze all aspects of corporate logistics to determine the most cost-effective or efficient means of transporting material or equipment. Conduct environmental audits for logistics activities based on storage, distribution, and transportation.

CUSTOMER SERVICE. Collaborate with other departments to integrate sales, order-management, accounting, shipping logistics, schedule meetings, perform reviews and interviews, and coordinate vehicle repairs and maintenance. Transmit and prioritize approved purchase orders and supporting documents to suppliers, vendors, or internal departments.

Accomplishment:

+ Spearheaded the development of an automated system for initiating action items to department heads. This system allowed for ongoing monitoring of action item status and report creation for executive staff. My efforts in designing, implementing, and maintaining this new system streamlined processes and resulted in a two-day reduction in response times while also increasing deadline compliance.

Supervisor: Kyle Bedlam (345-345-3456)
Okay to contact this Supervisor: Yes

Add your education as a "job block" to fill the period of time.

American Military University
N George St, Charles Town, WV 25414
Charles Town, WV   25414 United States

07/2011 - 05/2014
Hours per week: 30
Graduated - Bachelor's Level Student
Duties, Accomplishments and Related Skills:
Full - time Student with major in Philosophy.

US Army
1001 761st Tank Battalion Ave.
Fort Hood, TX   76544 United States

07/2009 - 10/2011
Salary: 4,500.00 USD Per Month
Hours per week: 40
SGT, 4th Combat Aviation Brigade, Task Force Comanche
Duties, Accomplishments and Related Skills:

ADMINISTRATIVE PROGRAM PLANNING. Composed memoranda for hazardous material transportation, record keeping for equipment and inventories, testing or training courses, and additional duty appointments using Microsoft Word. Created Microsoft Excel spreadsheets to track personnel, equipment, inventory, expiration dates, and procurement status.

ORAL & WRITTEN COMMUNICATION. Evaluated and wrote monthly performance and event counseling on 12 personnel using Lotus Forms viewer. Filed memoranda, performance reports, scheduled inventory and inspection results, and training records. Managed daily and monthly time keeping, coordination, and responsibilities of personnel.

DOCUMENT PREPARATION & REVIEW. Researched nomenclatures and product manuals for procurement of replacement and stock tools, equipment, and parts using Unit Level Logistics System-Aviation (Enhanced); enforced standard operating procedures for unit organization, resources, equipment, and personnel.

DATA TRACKING & REPORTING. Tracked mission-critical equipment using RFID tags and tracking software. Identified overdue items and maintenance schedules. Developed and updated Microsoft Excel spreadsheets for ordering and processing. Controlled compatibility of hazardous items transported and security requirements with special attention to U.S. and international laws and regulations.

PROJECT SCHEDULING. Scheduled hazardous material transportation and composed memoranda to alert constituents, kept detailed records for equipment and inventories, testing or training courses, and additional duty appointments using Microsoft Word. Monitored projected and delinquent calibration items list, liaised on-site and off-site management, and briefed Task Force Executive Officer of test, measurement, and diagnostic equipment status.

ADMINISTRATIVE & FINANCIAL SUPPORT. Created and maintained databases, documents and spreadsheets of procured items, tools, and equipment. Alerted supervisors to financial and material needs. Created Microsoft Excel spreadsheets to track equipment, inventory, acquisition dates, and procurement status.

AFTER RESUME: OUTLINE FORMAT / USAJOBS BUILDER

TRAINING & MENTORING. Supervised, counseled, trained, and mentored personnel on subject matter performance and event-orientations, special tools utilization, equipment distribution, and accountability. Serviced, maintained, and accounted for assigned equipment and provided support to Command on pre-deployment, deployment, and re-deployment accountability of personnel, equipment, and hazardous materials. Ensured financial and personnel readiness.

PROPERTY ACCOUNTABILITY. Responsible for property accountability for the Task Force tool room, conducted monthly and quarterly inventories, and provided status reports to the company Commander. Ensured compliance of Aviation Ground Support Equipment (AGSE) accountability and distribution standards for U.S. Army company.

Accomplishments:

+ Efficiently maintained the command library that consisted of Army Orders, Technical Instructions and Base Instructions. Conducted a major document review to identify relevant and outdated materials. Designed a database for document tracking and automated an audit process to ensure monthly review of all instructions. My efforts led to the elimination of more than 100 outdated instructions.

+ Received an "Outstanding Performance Award" for demonstrating knowledge of the policies and procedures pertaining to contracting and technical publications. Recognized with an "Exceptional Employee Award" for demonstrating an ability to motivate team members and keep projects on track, on schedule, and in regulatory compliance.

Supervisor: Thomas Bundy (123-123-1234)
Okay to contact this Supervisor: Yes

US Army, Pyeongtaek, South Korea
Camp Humphreys
APO, AP   96271 United States

07/2006 - 07/2009
Hours per week: 40
SGT, 2nd Combat Aviation Brigade
Duties, Accomplishments and Related Skills:

SUPERVISION & TEAM LEADERSHIP. Counseled, trained, and mentored personnel on subject matter performance, military education, and event-orientations; ensured financial and personal readiness. Assigned work schedules, evaluated performance, and adjusted resources based on mission needs.

PROCEDURAL KNOWLEDGE. Trained incoming personnel on maintenance, inspection, and flight procedures. Inspected and maintained 12 UH-60 helicopters for aero-medical company. Provided medical assistance to flight medic and visual guidance to pilots during training and real-life evacuation missions. Completed 24 real-world missions and received early promotions from Private 1st Class (E-3) to Specialist (E-4) (2007), and Specialist (E-4) to Sergeant (E-5) (2008).

MAINTENANCE & INSPECTIONS. Serviced and lubricated aircraft and subsystems and ensured aircraft met inspection and maintenance compliance. Performed scheduled inspections and assisted in special inspections, conducted limited maintenance operational checks, diagnosed, and troubleshot aircraft subsystems using special tools and equipment as required. Conducted maintenance on tools, special tools, and aircraft ground support equipment and drafted forms and records related to aircraft maintenance.

Accomplishment:
+ Non-Combatant Evacuation Operations (NEO) Warden - Participated in Non-Combatant Evacuation Operations (NEO) training exercises for South Korean peninsula. Researched documented members' compliance with NEO standards and equipment accountability, and inspected NEO equipment prior to distribution to ensure reliable operations.

Supervisor: Chuck Canoon (234-234-2345)
Okay to contact this Supervisor: Yes

Education: **American Military University** Charles Town, WV United States
Bachelor's Degree 05/2014
GPA: 3.9 of a maximum 4.0
Credits Earned: 122 Semester hours
Major: Philosophy **Honors:** Cum Laude
Relevant Coursework, Licenses and Certifications:
Proficiency in Writing; Effectiveness in Writing; Research, Analysis, and Writing; International Relations; Social Problems; Social Change; Women of Color: A Cross-Cultural Comparison; Logic; Ethical Theories and Concepts; Contemporary Issues in Philosophy; Enlightenment Philosophy; Modern and Post-modern Philosophy; Ethics in Criminal Justice; Management Ethics; Moral Issues in Health Care; Environmental Ethics; Epistemology; Senior Seminar in Philosophy

MAJOR PROJECTS

PHIL498 Senior Seminar - Philosophy Capstone Course
- The purpose of the senior seminar is to conduct intensive research on a topic of philosophy integrating the knowledge acquired from previous philosophy courses. The research topic was a personal ethic referred to as The Principle of Nonmaleficence, which discusses the state of an initial moral status where one does not inflict evil or do harm to others. The 12-page discourse includes subjects and theories stemming from medical ethics, political philosophy, and environmental ethics.

SOCI403 Social Change – Sociology
- In the course of eight weeks, I partook in a three-stage writing assignment research paper that included structuring a topic; an annotated bibliography; and the full body essay collaborating the causes, patterns, and trends associated with social change. The topic explains how work stigma affects some ways that societies negatively view unemployed, underemployed, and overqualified workers or students from a multidimensional perspective, which includes economic, academic, and cultural ideologies.

WOMS400 Women of Color: A Cross-Cultural Comparison – Women's Studies
- This course examines global women of color from underdeveloped, developing, and developed nations, and various cultural, ethnic, historical, anthropological, and sociological theories and perspectives, which focus on gender inequity and stratification.

Job Related   Technical Transportation of Hazardous Material
Training: March 2010

UH-60 Helicopter Repairer Course (15T10)
March 2006 - June 2006

AFTER RESUME: OUTLINE FORMAT / USAJOBS BUILDER CONT.

VETERAN CASE STUDY: MARIANO TORY

Language Skills:

Language	Spoken	Written	Read
Spanish	Intermediate	Intermediate	Intermediate

Affiliations:

National Society of Collegiate Scholars - VP of Community Services
Student Veterans of America - Member
Second Infantry Division Association - Member
Golden Key International Honor Society - Member

References:

Name	Employer	Title	Phone	Email
Thomas Bundy	US Army	Sergeant First Class	111-111-1111	Thomas.bundy@mail.mil
Chris Wash	United States Army	Staff Sergeant	222-222-2222	c-wash@yahoo.com
Kent Mestnick	Northwest Public University System	Professor	333-333-3333	Kent.mestnick@nw.psys.edu

Additional Information:

AWARDS AND ACHIEVEMENTS
United States Army September 2006 – November 2011
Army Commendation Medals
Army Achievement Medals
Army Good Conduct Medal
National Defense Service Medal
Korean Defense Service Medal
Afghanistan Campaign Medal (with Service Star)
Global War on Terrorism Service Medal
Non-Commissioned Officer Professional Development Ribbon
Army Service Ribbon, Overseas Service Ribbon
NATO Medal
Certificate of Achievement
Aviation Badge; Recommended for promotions (2007, 2008, and 2011)
Sikorsky Aircraft Rescue Award

INTERESTS AND HOBBIES
Information Technology: Diagnosing, troubleshooting, and servicing personal computers by enhancing or installing software, installing or replacing hardware, downloading necessary updates, removing viruses, spyware, and malware; Physical fitness: Running and Calisthenics; Firearm proficiency; Automotive maintenance and performance; Reading; Self-improvement; French language

BEFORE RESUME: BULLET FORMAT

Bobbi is a U.S. Navy military spouse and Program S registrant seeking a career in military transition while her husband is pursuing a U.S. Navy career.

BOBBI ROBINS

1020 Edmund Ave. • Baltimore, MD 21228
555-555-5555 • bobbir@gmail.com

PROFESSIONAL SUMMARY

Ten years of customer service experience. Continuously awarded highest possible ratings on performance reviews, willing to travel, able to maintain a flexible schedule. Seven years' experience with organizing and disseminating large amounts of data to students, families, Marines, and Sailors. Proficient in Microsoft (MS) Word, MS Excel, MS Outlook, MS PowerPoint, MS Publisher, Naval Correspondence, Adobe Acrobat and SharePoint.

EDUCATION

B.A. (Asian Studies), University of Maryland University College, Okinawa, Japan, 2011
B.A. (Psychology; Human Development Minor), State University of New York College at Geneseo, New York, 2008

WORK AND VOLUNTEER EXPERIENCES

Family Readiness Assistant   **Jul 2009 – Present**
Marine Corps Family Team Building (Okinawa, Japan and Ft. Meade, MD)

- Volunteered organizational and communication aid to the Family Readiness Officers (FRO) for Combat Logistic Regiment 37, the 31st Marine Expeditionary Unit (MEU), 3d Reconnaissance Battalion and currently Marine Cryptologic Support Battalion.
- Made telephone calls to welcome new families to the unit.
- Assisted with quarterly newsletter for 3d Recon Battalion and monthly newsletters for the MEU.
- Help with the promotion and evaluation of unit events and workshops via spouse-based feedback.
- Assist with administrative duties such as reconciling rosters and service members' documentation.

Lifestyle, Insight, Networking, Knowledge, Skills (L.I.N.K.S). Mentor   **Feb 2012 – Jun 2013**
Marine Corps Family Team Building (Okinawa, Japan)

- Briefed 1-2 assigned sections of the L.I.N.K.S. curriculum at monthly workshops for up to 40 participants.
- Coordinated appropriate activities to accompany oral instruction of L.I.N.K.S. materials.

Family Readiness Officer   **Nov 2009 – Jan 2013**
Marine Corps Family Team Building (Okinawa, Japan)

- Served at the battalion and regimental levels as the Commanding Officer's (CO) representative for Unit, Personal, and Family Readiness Program (UPFRP) outreach.
- Provided support and assistance to Marines, Sailors, and their families through weekly informational email communications and newsletters, monthly target-specific educational workshops, and biannual family events.
- Used MS Excel, MS Outlook, and Marine Online to maintain distribution lists of up to 750 Marines spread throughout up to six companies and their family members; used distribution lists to facilitate home and section visits as well as telephone, post, and email communications in order to maximize awareness of the UPFRP and to connect eligible persons with needed support services.
- Coordinated presence of program resource specialists at major unit events to increase accessibility.
- Conducted biannual surveys to assess needs of families and personnel to increase the program's value.
- Provided the CO with weekly informational updates on the UPFRP via email or brief and hosted monthly Command Team meetings for information dissemination and program activity coordination.

- Interviewed and supervised eleven Family Readiness Assistants and Command Team Advisors as well as coordinated annual volunteer recognitions from the CO and recognition at unit events.
- Utilized various software-based systems, such as SharePoint and resource websites, to gather resource information for inclusion in the weekly email; used MS Word to develop and publish a weekly newsletter that reflected this information and accompanied these emails; built and maintained the unit's eMarine website to serve as an additional reference point for current information.
- Managed annual Unit Family Readiness Funds budgets of up to $17,000, allocated funds and donated items and ensured that spending was within the guidelines stipulated for Non-Appropriated Funds.
- Fostered support systems for new and less experienced FROs through mentorship.
- Created marketing flyers and mailing postcards using MS Word and MS Publisher to promote awareness of targeted unit trainings and gatherings, such as pre-deployment briefs.
- Organized monthly workshops for families in order to increase readiness, resiliency, and to encourage investment in the community.
- Organized quarterly workshops and annual trainings for Marines to increase readiness and improve resource awareness.
- Provided extra support to families during the seven off-island exercises that required participation from the battalion and the regiment via briefs on available services and benefits and extra outreach.

CPR/AED/First Aid/Babysitters' Course Instructor Jul 2011 – Jun 2013
American Red Cross (Okinawa, Japan)

- Taught cardiopulmonary resuscitation (CPR) and basic first aid to adults and teens in monthly classes of up to ten students; also provided instruction on operation of an automated external defibrillator (AED).
- Conducted monthly babysitters' classes for up to 10 teens and pre-teens on how to properly care for infants and children.

English Teacher Jul 2009 – Nov 2012
Y.M.A.K. Institute (Okinawa, Japan)

- Developed lesson plans and conversational dialog examples in order to instruct 15 adult Japanese professionals in weekly conversational English and English grammar classes.
- Established an intensive English course for young adults in transition to overseas employment.
- Prepared monthly quizzes and motivated students to learn and practice English through interaction and discussion. These motivational practices increased student performance on quizzes and their understanding of the English language by 60 percent since July 2009.

Website Administrator and Newsletter Editor Aug 2010 – Jun 2012
Marine Officers' Spouses' Club of Okinawa (Okinawa, Japan)

- Promoted monthly Marine Officers' Spouse's Club of Okinawa events that supported the funding of local charities by updating the Facebook page, the website, and the quarterly newsletter.
- Created, edited, and distributed newsletters using MS Publisher and Homestead web hosting software.
- Obtained member-run business and outside organization advertisements.
- Electronically distributed the quarterly newsletter to more than 300 members of the organization in order to increase participation in club events, present the quarter's charitable donations, and to maximize the amount of time that advertisers had their information on display.

AFTER RESUME: OUTLINE FORMAT / UPLOAD

BOBBI ROBINS

1020 Edmund Ave. • Baltimore, MD 21228
555-555-5555 • bobbir@gmail.com
Military Spouse • U.S. Citizen

CAREER OBJECTIVES: Social Services Series, GS-0101-07/09; Administration and Program Series, GS-0301-07/09; Program Management Series, GS-0340-07/09.

SUMMARY OF SKILLS:
Six years' experience in employment readiness counseling, case management, employment training coordination, and database maintenance. Specialized knowledge in federal employment, military spouse and veterans' preference for federal careers. Effective webinar instructor and training coordinator. Effective in customer service, attention to detail and follow-up. Proficient in information databases: Adobe Quickbase, Excel, Google Doc management; gotomeeting.com systems; Constant Contact updates; mail-merge, survey development and study tracking systems.

PROFESSIONAL EXPERIENCE

EMPLOYMENT SERVICES AND TRAINING COORDINATOR   **02/2014 – Present**
Federal Career Training Institute and The Resume Place, Inc., Catonsville, MD   40 Hours per Week
1012 Edmondson Avenue, Catonsville, MD 21228
Supervisor: Kathryn Troutman, (410) 744-4324; may contact

FEDERAL EMPLOYMENT READINESS CONSULTANT: Review client resumes and federal job targets to determine congruence among their eligibility, career goals, and the target job field. Counsel students, private industry clients, current federal employees, military veterans, and spouse clients on their career objectives and direct them towards federal job resources.

CLIENT ASSIGNMENT: Oversee federal resume case management, encompassing a range of clientele seeking consulting, training, and writing services for federal employment. Review client objectives and clarify the scope of work purchased. Evaluate workloads, schedules, and writer specialties to assign projects to 20+ professional staff.

TRAINING COORDINATOR, TEN STEPS TO A FEDERAL JOB®: Coordinate registrations; provide training support, materials delivery for military and university career and employment counselors worldwide.   Follow-up after live and webinar trainings to manage evaluations, materials and Ten Steps material distribution. Produce invoices and discuss Ten Steps training program materials and resources with purchase officers.

WEBINAR INSTRUCTOR: Using gotomeeting.com technology, teach 30-minute webinars to federal applicants, including Ten Steps to a Federal Job™. Coordinate and act as facilitator for webinar series with other panelists. Set up webinar classes online and provide PowerPoints and handouts for webinar classes. Manage course evaluations.

MAINTAIN CLIENT AND TRAINING DATABASES: Using Adobe QuickBase and Excel in Google docs, maintain annual certifications and ensure that registrations and licenses are maintained. For resume service clients, maintain the same database for client information, documents, project estimates and assignments. Follow through to ensure data is up-to-date.

PROJECT MANAGEMENT: Team Leader for a major project aimed at leveraging resources and technology to improve client tracking and success rates. Conduct data analysis across multiple databases and collaborate with staff to revise reporting procedures. Develop customer satisfaction surveys and coordinate ongoing work standardization efforts.

CUSTOMER SERVICE: Deliver high-quality support and service to all customers through effective communication, tactfulness, and a professional demeanor. Provide project cost estimates and interact with clients via phone, email, and other written correspondence. Manage and resolve client complaints, and coordinate with staff members and subcontractors to ensure client satisfaction.

Key Accomplishments:

- Improved communication with past Ten Steps Certified trainers through updated correspondence to support our three year Ten Steps License.
- Supported the creation of a database that tracked the Ten Steps classes being taught worldwide by licensed trainers and the number of classes taught per base. Recognized that more than 226 military bases were licensed to teach Ten Steps to a Federal Job in 2012; and more than 12,000 of the Ten Steps text – Jobseeker's Guide – were supporting the Ten Steps curriculum. Created new data to recognize the importance of federal employment training for military spouses, transitioning military and civilians.
- Improved resume client database system to improve tracking, customer service data and client results information. Designed a survey and received results from 140 federal resume clients.

FAMILY READINESS OFFICER (NF-0301-04) 11/2009 – 02/2013
Marine Corps Community Services, Camp Schwab, Okinawa, Japan 40 Hours per Week
Supervisor: Taylor Sophreti, xxx-xxx-xxxx; may contact

CLIENT SUPPORT & NEEDS ASSESSMENTS: Conducted biannual surveys to assess needs of families and personnel to increase the program's value. Assisted clients in prioritizing issues/developing plans and goals tailored to meet specific needs. Provided support and assistance to the Marines, Sailors, and their families through weekly informational email communications and newsletters.

WORK & FAMILY LIFE EXPERT: Managed the presence of program resource specialists at major unit events to increase accessibility. Fostered support systems for new and less experienced FROs through mentorship. Connected outbound personnel and family members with FROs at their gaining command.

VOLUNTEER RECRUITMENT AND COORDINATION: Interviewed and supervised a team of 11 Family Readiness Assistants and Command Team Advisors. Coordinated annual volunteer recognition events.

COMMUNICATION MANAGEMENT: Used MS Excel, MS Outlook, and Marine Online to maintain distribution lists of up to 750 Marines spread throughout six companies and their family members. Used distribution lists to facilitate home and section visits as well as telephone, post, and email communications to maximize awareness of the program and to connect eligible persons with needed support services.

CONDUCTED INTERVIEWS: Conducted interviews to establish the nature and extent of concerns and issues posed by military family members. Provided assistance in developing personal and family-based goals and plans. Collaborated with social service delivery systems in the military and civilian community to manage clients and ensure positive results.

FINANCIAL MANAGEMENT & ADVICE: Managed annual Unit Family Readiness budgets of up to $17,000. Allocated funds and donated items while ensuring that spending stayed within the guidelines stipulated for Non-Appropriated Funds. Provided the Commander with weekly informational updates on the program's financial status.

NEWSLETTER WRITING & EDITING: Utilized various software-based systems, such as SharePoint and resource websites, to gather information for inclusion in the weekly email. Used MS Word to develop and publish a weekly newsletter. Built and maintained the unit's e-Marine website to serve as an additional reference point.

AFTER RESUME: OUTLINE FORMAT / UPLOAD CONT.

Key Accomplishments:

- As a Family Readiness Officer at Camp Schwab, Okinawa, Japan, it was my responsibility to coordinate efforts to celebrate the unit's children. I suggested that the children of the local children's home and orphanage, the Nagomi Children's Home in Henoko, come to the Military Family Day. I also coordinated with the American Red Cross to collect items that would be useful to the children in the home, as well as blankets and toys. As a result of my efforts, seventeen children and five caregivers from the children's home participated in the event along with 28 American service and family members. This was the first unit-initiated event of its kind and the first real cultural exchange opportunity for many of the families in attendance.

- Coordinated with FROs across the 3d Marine Division and other outside organizations, such as the Camp Courtney Junior Marines, to plan and execute the first-ever annual 3d Marine Division Marine Corps Birthday Ball for Kids.

VOLUNTEER EXPERIENCE

FAMILY READINESS ASSISTANT (VOLUNTEER)   **07/2009 – 06/2013**
Marine Corps Community Services, Okinawa, Japan   10 Hours per Week
Supervisor: Carl Handers, xxx-xxx-xxxx; may contact

FAMILY READINESS EXPERT: Directly supported and assisted the Family Readiness Officer (FRO) in managing the Unit Family Readiness Program. Applied in-depth knowledge of the Commander's family readiness goals and proactively coordinated with military members and their families to increase morale and quality of life. Advised on military organization, lifestyle issues, and stresses accompanying military life to enhance relationships.

Key Accomplishment:
- Successfully responded to a need for improved communication with Marines and their family members by revamping the design and content of both weekly and monthly newsletters. My efforts directly resulted in a redesigned communication campaign that was buoyed by a visually enhanced publication and a more welcoming tone.

L.I.N.K.S. MENTOR (VOLUNTEER)   **02/2012 – 06/2013**
Marine Corps Community Services, Okinawa, Japan   10 Hours per Week
Supervisor: Bruce Sandtople, xxx-xxx-xxxx; may contact

INDIVIDUAL & TEAM MENTORING: Worked on a one-on-one and team basis to mentor service members and their families on the benefits, resources, and services available. Provided mentorship and guidance across Lifestyle, Insights, Networking, Knowledge, and Skills (LINKS).

CLASS INSTRUCTION: Instructed classes and workshops on a range of topics encompassing the military lifestyle. Delivered information at awareness/briefing sessions and presented key points to specifically targeted audiences, such as parents, children, spouses, etc. Briefed 1-2 assigned sections of the curriculum at monthly workshops of up to 40 participants.

EDUCATION

BACHELOR OF ARTS (B.A.) – 2011
University of Maryland University College
Major: Asian Studies • GPA: 3.82

BACHELOR OF ARTS (B.A.) – 2008
State University of New York at Geneseo
Major: Psychology & Human Development • GPA: 3.34

PROFESSIONAL TRAINING

Certified Federal Job Search Trainer / Certified Federal Career Coach, Federal Career Training Institute, certified Ten Steps to a Federal Job™ Trainer, June 2013 – June 2016.
L.I.N.K.S. Mentor Training (2012) • Level I Active Military Families Facilitator (2011) • Four Lenses Facilitator (2011) • SharePoint End User (2010) • Seven Habits of Highly Effective Families (2010)

TECHNICAL SKILLS

Microsoft Office Suite (Word, Excel, PowerPoint, Access) • Statistical Package for Social Sciences (SPSS) • QuickBooks • QuickBase • SharePoint • e-Marine • Marine Online

SPOUSE PREFERENCE

Spouse of Active Duty USMC. Eligible for consideration under Executive Order 13473, September 11, 2009 Non-competitive Appointment for Certain Military Spouses, and DoD Priority Placement Program.

BEFORE RESUME: BIG BLOCK

Bill is a non-disabled vet (TP) separated from U.S. Army Reserves with a complicated Reserves resume with civilian experience. He landed a great Contract Specialist career ladder position.

BILL NETHERS
Baltimore, MD
410 744 4444
bill.nethers@gmail.com

PROFESSIONAL EXPERIENCE

FT. BELVOIR, VA, 2012-Present, Recovering from injuries sustained in Iraq

UNITED STATES ARMY – Baltimore, MD, 2011, Photojournalist
Responsible for providing photographic documentation of military events for a unit consisting of 40 personnel; captured key moments from award ceremonies, presentations, and graduations. Utilized digital camera, tripod, filters and flash for events and interviews. Accountable for cameras and equipment valued in excess of $10K with zero losses or discrepancies. Developed composition, interviewed and selected interviewees, and added lighting for desired effects. Created artificial light as needed to match the required photography elements for Defense Media print and online publications. Researched Iraqi military history and US military actions write informative news items. Utilized judgment and active listening to select interviewees for military and Defense Dept. musical presentations. Researched composers, musical selections, venues and historical venues for publications. Authored 2 published articles, covering the progress and transition for an Iraqi Award Ceremony. For the Iraqi Award Ceremony, researched the history of the Iraqi war, events, military leaders and the transition plans. The US Army Band performed both Iraqi and America military popular selections for an important and somber celebration of the war in Iraq. Submitted the article to several defense media organizations, received edits and comments, and rewrote and edited both content and selection of photographs based on publisher/ managing editor requests. Covered all high profile events of visiting US dignitaries in Iraq. Scheduled, researched background and lead interviews with US Dignitaries in Iraq.

Army Band Leader – Baltimore, MD, 2005 – 2010
Managed a musical ensemble of 3 personnel, responsible for the scheduling or practices and performances for the Blues Band events. Direct groups at rehearsals and live or recorded performances. Plan and schedule rehearsals and performances. Arrange details such as locations, accompanists and instrumentalists. Write concert notes, bios for performers, and coordinate production of concert playbills. Study scores to rehearse and select instrumentalists for special programs. Utilize technology such as digital interfaces, sequencers, music sound editing equipment. Study scores to learn music in detail and to develop interpretations. Communicate with supply chain planners to review availability. Analyze and maintain music and equipment inventory. Designed a new method of organizing more than 7,000 items of musical scores into music genres, solos, composers and frequency of performance (dates). Responsible for strategic planning, resource allocation, human resources (band members and staff – 20 members total) planning, leadership of the musicians, and coordination of specialty bands and resources. Accountable for $15K in equipment and musical instruments. Resolve problems concerning transportation, logistics and equipment set-up. Collaborate with band members, base or concert site labor and management, and packaging of equipment. Maintain customer service and shipping logs. Maintain safety reports for equipment set-up, concert venue safety. Supervise logistics team and schedulers. Direct inbound and outbound logistics, inventory maintenance and supplies. With limited budget, contracted with Appalachian Blue Grass for

best price for musical instruments and equipment. Resulted in cost savings for the band multiple times.. Performed additional duties for grounds and instrument maintenance/ Assisted in the construction and maintenance of the band library and supply room, reorganizing supply storage of equipment. Performed in the Rock Band as a guitar player and a percussionist in the Concert Band. Performed over 50 musical performances throughout the United States. Stood up the Army Blues Band to increase greater range of concert venues and revenues. Increased band member morale by offering 25% more band and concert venues and contributed to musician performance opportunities. Facilitated the retention of top performers in the Army Band.

APPALACHIAN BLUE GRASS– Catonsville, MD, 2004 – 2010, Guitar Department Manager
Planned and prioritized Guitar Department purchasing activities. Reviewed proposed seasonal and yearly orders, generated purchase requisition orders, and assist the owner in the approval process. Prioritized and submitted standing purchase orders and related documentation to over ten vendors. Supervised 4 sales associates, responsible for ensuring excellent customer service and sales operations. Organized and tracked order acknowledgments, recorded and communicated inventory shortages and backorders. Tracked all guitar department orders, confirmed system lead times, and monitored projected delivery dates and relative costs. Reviewed, updated and followed through with purchase requisition orders until they are closed out. Pursued Vendor merchandise sales, and created qualifying purchase requisition orders to receive maximum discounts on tiered level product pricing. Organized and tracked order acknowledgments, recorded and communicated inventory shortages and backorders. Tracked all guitar department orders, confirmed system lead times, and monitored projected delivery dates and relative costs. Reviewed, updated and followed through with purchase requisition orders until they are closed out. Pursued Vendor merchandise sales, and created qualifying purchase requisition orders to receive maximum discounts on tiered level product pricing. Worked with the store owner to ensure orders comply with vendor agreements and contracts, and report on visible compliance issues. Established relationships with school and individual customers for musical band, orchestra and individual performance requests. Persuaded customer who came in to buy $7 guitar strings to purchase $3,000+ guitar. Prepared operational reports regarding sales, inventory, staff, and government sales as a Small Business contractor to the US Army Band. Provided customer services for musicians, including instrument demonstrations, recommendations for performance and education plans, and payment plans for equipment purchases. Negotiated with band and orchestra directors and school and government purchasing agents for bulk equipment orders and deliveries. Responsible for ordering all merchandise for guitar department, managing a quarterly budget of $70K. Accountable for over $700K in guitar merchandise. Successfully discovered large discrepancy of sheet music and discovered that the music manufacturer miscounted when shipping to our store. Identified serial shoplifter from video surveillance tapes after noticing inventory shortages. Confronted perpetrator and forced him to return stolen equipment and agree to never return. Utilized bar code readers and supervise regular inventory taking and reports for corporate office. Researched discrepancies. Performed register operations, cash, credit, check. Managed store layout, manufacturer sales materials, equipment display in a 25,000 sf storefront retail operation. Trained staff in equipment, manufacturers, warranties, Achieved number one Fender Custom Shop Guitar dealer in the State of Maryland three years consecutively.

EDUCATION / CERTIFICATIONS: A.A. General Studies, Catonsville Community College, MD, 2012; Non-Commissioned Officer leadership training; Access Data Certified Examiner

AWARDS: 4 Army Achievement Medals; Maryland Achievement Medal; Iraqi Campaign Medal; Global War on Terrorism Service Medal; Non-Commissioned Officer Professional Development Ribbon

STEP 6 | AFTER RESUME: OUTLINE FORMAT / UPLOAD

BILL NETHERS

6787 Foxhill Road
Baltimore, MD
410 744 4444
bill.nethers@gmail.com

OBJECTIVE:
Acquisition Directorate Workforce Program (W2W)

QUALIFICATIONS

Proven acquisitions / purchasing experience as Department Manager, Appalachian Blue Grass, 2004 to 2010. Experience in negotiations, vendor relations, government contracts and purchasing and supply management services.

PROFESSIONAL EXPERIENCE

WOUNDED WARRIOR (E-6, Staff Sergeant)   **09/2011 - 01/2014**
Army National Guard Warrior Transition Unit, Ft. Belvoir, VA   Salary: $71,416
Supervisor: SSG Ron Smith (333) 333-3333, may contact   40 hours/week

Earned cum laude Associate of Science Degree in General Studies, 2012. Relevant courses: Principles of Microeconomics; Introduction to Business; Introduction to Computer Applications and Concepts; Math for Liberal Arts; Intercultural Communication. Received Medical Discharge and separated from the Maryland Army National Guard as an E-6, Staff Sergeant, in Jan. 2014.

PHOTOJOURNALIST (E-5)   **05/2011 - 09/2011**
Maryland Army National Guard, Camp Liberty, Baghdad, Iraq   Salary: $71,416
Supervisor: N/A   40 hours/week

Volunteered for deployment to Iraq with 29th Maryland Army National Guard Public Affairs Division. Maintained accountability for cameras and equipment valued in excess of $10,000 with zero losses or discrepancies.

ARMY BAND LEADER (E-5)   **05/2005 - 12/2010**
Army National Guard, Baltimore, MD   Salary: $71,416
Supervisor: SSG Tom Williams 443-333-3333, may contact   40 hours/week

BAND LEADER: Managed and performed in Blues Band musical ensemble of three personnel as part of Maryland Army National Guard 229th Army Band. Also participated in Rock Band and Concert Band. Played 50+ musical performances at National Guard and civilian public outreach events nationwide one weekend per month and two weeks in the summer.

ASSISTANT SUPPLY SERGEANT: Oversaw logistics arrangements and personnel transportation for upwards of 20 staff, managed inventory and accountability, oversaw general and equipment maintenance for the unit, helped build and maintain Band Library and Supply Room, and reorganized supply storage area. Consistently accounted for up to $100,000 in equipment and musical instruments with zero discrepancies.

ACCOMPLISHENTS:

- Creatively overcame limited funds for procurement of musical instruments by leveraging my civilian position as a Manager with Appalachian Blue Grass music shop, Catonsville, MD to help the Army Band procure needed instruments at cost multiple times, releasing cost savings to the Band for other equipment or supplies.
- Stood up the Army Blues Band on my own initiative to offer wider variety of music and satisfy greater range of clients. Enabled the Band to secure new venues and augment existing venues. Increased Army Band morale by allowing members to contribute to their full potential and develop professionally. Facilitated retention of key musicians who otherwise would have left the Army Band.

DEPARTMENT MANAGER   07/2004 - 12/2010
Appalachian Blue Grass, Catonsville, MD   Salary: $33,138
Supervisor: Sam Smith 443-333-3333, may contact   40 hours/week

PURCHASING ACTIVITIES: Planned and prioritized Guitar Department purchasing activities. Reviewed proposed seasonal and yearly orders, generated purchase requisition orders, and assisted the owner in the approval process. Prioritized and submitted standing purchase orders and related documentation to over ten vendors.

TRACKED ORDERS AND INVENTORY SHORTAGES: Organized and tracked order acknowledgments; recorded and communicated inventory shortages and backorders. Tracked all guitar department orders, confirmed system lead times, and monitored projected delivery dates and relative costs.

NEGOTIATED WITH VENDORS: Pursued vendor merchandise sales, and created qualifying purchase requisition orders to receive maximum discounts on tiered level product pricing. Worked with the store owner to ensure orders comply with vendor agreements and contracts, and reported on visible compliance issues.

INVOICE REVIEWS AND NEGOTIATED COST SAVINGS: Reported invoice discrepancies to the owner and worked with finance to provide documentation to resolve reception. Achieved efficient business transactions and significant cost savings by identifying opportunities.

VENDOR RELATIONS: Worked with three vendors to design popular guitar products, while finding ways to reduce cost through model based backdoors while adhering to period correct specifications and quality. Achieved number one Fender Custom Shop Guitar dealer in the State of Maryland three years consecutively.

GUITAR DEPARTMENT MANAGER: Supervised four sales associates, ensured excellent customer service, and oversaw sales operations at one of the area's largest and busiest music stores. Oversaw, managed, and performed guitar and amplifier repairs. Ordered all merchandise for guitar department and managed quarterly budget of $70,000.

ACCOMPLISHMENTS:
- Advised the owner to establish small-business contracting schedule with the General Service Administration (GSA) to sell the best price guitars and musical instruments to the Army Reserves Band.
- Maintained accountability for $700,000+ in guitar merchandise and up to $70,000 in annual sales with zero discrepancies.

AFTER RESUME: OUTLINE FORMAT / UPLOAD CONT.

WOUNDED WARRIOR CASE STUDY: BILL NETHERS

- Repeatedly used my knowledge and dedication to excellent customer service to convince customers to choose best-available instruments. Persuaded customer who came in to buy $7 guitar strings to purchase $3,000+ guitar.
- Identified serial shoplifter from video surveillance tapes after noticing inventory shortages. Confronted perpetrator and forced him to return stolen equipment and agree to never return.

EDUCATION / CERTIFICATIONS

Access Data Certified Examiner, 04/2013.
A.A., Cum Laude, General Studies, Catonsville Community College, Catonsville, MD, 08/2012.
Non-Commissioned Officer Warrior Leadership Training, Ft. Indiantown Gap, PA, 05/2010.

MILITARY SERVICE

U.S. National Guard:
Washington, DC National Guard, 10/2000-09/2001, 05/2004-05/2005
Maryland National Guard, 05/2005-01/2014

Highest rank achieved: E-6, Staff Sergeant. Received Honorable Medical Discharge, 01/2014. Overseas deployment, Iraq, 2011.

U.S. Army:

U.S. Army, 08/1993-02/1997, highest rank: E-3. Stationed in Germany with OPFOR Division (training unit); Ft. Bliss, TX, Headquarters Brigade, Air Defense Artillery Directorate. At Ft. Bliss, served as driver and assistant to Commanding Officer. Transported CO and senior dignitaries, and helped organize CO's schedule.

AWARDS

4 Army Achievement Medals: 2009, 2014
Army Commendation Medal
State of MD Commendation Medal, 2011
Iraqi Campaign Medal with Campaign Star
Global War on Terrorism Service Medal

2 Army Good Conduct Medals
4 Army Reserve Achievement Medals
Non-Commissioned Officer Professional
Development Ribbon
2 Overseas Service Ribbons

WOUNDED WARRIOR RESUME TRANSITION DESCRIPTIONS | STEP 6

If you are a Wounded Warrior, it can be tricky to figure out how to write about your recovery and rehabilitation time in your federal resume. Because each individual utilizes the Wounded Warrior Program in different ways, here are five suggestions on how to include your program activities in your federal resume.

1. Include a Short Description

WORK HISTORY:

USMC Wounded Warrior Regiment, West, Camp Pendleton, CA (Feb. 2013 to April 2014)
Active Duty, E-5. Completed one year of medical, rehabilitative recovery, reconditioning, counseling and transition training in order to achieve wellness. Achieved a level of success to seek transition into civilian life.

2. Include Internships

USMC Wounded Warrior Regiment, West (12/2014 to present)
Active Duty, E-5, Camp Pendleton, CA

- Completed one year of medical, rehabilitative recovery, reconditioning, counseling and transition training in order to achieve wellness. Achieved a level of success to seek transition into civilian life.

- Successfully completed 3 internships while balancing work schedule with medical appointments and clinic visits (physical therapy sessions, and prosthetic related appointments).

HR Intern (September 2014–November 2014)
TriCare, San Diego, CA

SUPPORT HR ACTIVITIES: Attended and contributed to strategy meetings in an effort to refine the existing internship program. Worked closely with the Diversity and Inclusion Manager to share ideas and exchange program information.

Office Clerk/Intern (August 2014–October 2014)
Congressman Clark Kent's Office, San Diego, CA

REPORT GENERATION AND ADMINISTRATIVE SUPPORT: Created and maintained calendars, identifying and resolving any potential scheduling conflicts.

Talent Acquisition & Development Military Program Intern (April 2014–July 2014)
Genuine Education, San Diego, CA

3. Show Education and Training

> ### PROFESSIONAL EXPERIENCE
>
> **WOUNDED WARRIOR, E-5**   09/2013-Present
> Warrior Transition Unit, Ft. Belvoir, VA   40 hours/week
> Supervisor: SSgt Herbie Polo, 555-555-5555, may contact
>
> **Undergoing intensive regimen of medical treatment and physical rehabilitation** after suffering service-connected injuries in Iraq, 07/2011. Actively transitioning to civilian life, including by:
> - **Earned cum laude Associate of Science Degree** in General Studies, 2012. Relevant courses: Principles of Microeconomics; Introduction to Business; Introduction to Computer Applications and Concepts; Math for Liberal Arts; Intercultural Communication.
> - **Earned Access Data Certified Examiner**, 04/2013; completed 40-hour Digital Forensics course.
> - **Completed additional Northern Virginia Community College course:** Introduction to Geospatial Imaging, 2013.
> - **Developing knowledge** of Federal civilian employment process, including resume writing, skills translation, job series, application processes, and available employment resources.

4. Highlight Transition Skills Training

> **USCG Wounded Warrior, E-5**   09/2014 – Present
> **Walter Reed National Military Medical Center**   Salary: $71.416
> Bethesda, Maryland   40 hours / week
>
> WOUNDED WARRIOR REGIMENT: Participate in the Wounded Warrior Regiment which provides and facilitates assistance to wounded, ill, and injured military attached to or in support of USCG units, and their family members in order to assist them as they return to duty or transition to civilian life.
>
> TRANSITION SKILLS DEVELOPMENT: Through comprehensive web-based employment toolbox, learn about: resume writing, skills translation, networking; transition courses; job placement; vocational rehabilitation; and specific guidance through the employment process by providing a range of employment resources and referral information.
>
> KEY ACCOMPLISHMENTS: Learning how to strengthen myself from the inside out through special programs which show skills in how to improve overall self-esteem, self-confidence, and self-worth. Fully participate in: leadership, mentorship, lines of operation, individual and unit athletics, and community service events and activities.
>
> REASON FOR LEAVING: Regained strength and abilities to return to work and life after the military. Transition date is December 31, 2013. I will be relocating to Bethesda, MD and separating from the USCG as an E-5 seeking a new career in Investigative Support Services. I am flexible about the location of my next employment. I am seeking a full-time position.

5. Almost Hidden

FOOD SERVICE SPECIALIST

Dynamic and hard-working food service professional with extensive experience in preparing and serving food, workplace sanitation, menu planning, and customer service. Proven team builder who exhibits decisiveness and leadership under pressure. Demonstrated ability to prioritize tasks and meet deadlines. Excellent public speaking and interpersonal skills. Proven customer service skills with diverse customers. Experience working as a Food Service Specialist for the United States Marine Corps. ***Currently in the Wounded Warrior Transition Program, NIH (08/2014 – Present).***

CAREER HISTORY AND HIGHLIGHTS

United States Marine Corps -
2013 – 2014
12th Marine Chow Hall
Camp Hansen, Okinawa, Japan
■ **Food Service Specialist**
- Procured, prepared, stored and distributed food for troop consumption.
- Oversaw menu and recipe planning; meal preparation and serving; sanitation; operation and management of facilities and personnel; training; and accounting and reporting functions for garrison and field operations.
- Handled the funding, requisitioning, purchasing, receiving, and accounting for sustenance supplies.
- Provided quality assurance surveillance procedures for food processing, mess hall operations, and storage facilities.

Pursuing Passion Led to Success

"A Wounded Warrior wanted to go into IT, but it wasn't his passion. He was just chasing the dollar. I asked him what he really enjoyed and had experience in. He told me it was dog training. There was a vacancy for that, and he got the job.

"By looking into their passion, the Wounded Warrior can end up doing something that they really enjoy doing. They can stay in the occupation for years to come, because they have a passion for it."

-- Dennis Eley, MBA, Regional Wounded Warrior Coordinator at the OCHR San Diego Operations Center

The Factor Evaluation System (FES) is part of the Classification Standards and includes nine factors that are part of most nonsupervisory GS positions. These descriptions are used for assigning grades under the GS system and are highly useful for improving your resume.

Look through the FES definitions in the Classification Standard for your target position. Where applicable, add the answers to the following key FES questions into your resume to dramatically improve your federal resume content.

KNOWLEDGE

- What knowledge do you have to help you do your job?

SUPERVISORY CONTROLS

- What kind of supervisory control do you have?
- Or do you work independently?

GUIDELINES USED

- What guidelines do you use to do your job?
- What laws, regulations or references?
- List all legislation, manuals, SOPs, policies, references

COMPLEXITY

- How complex are the duties of your position?

SCOPE & EFFECT

- Who do you talk to and work with?
- What is the scope of your work?
- Is it local, regional, worldwide?

PERSONAL CONTACTS AND PURPOSE OF CONTACTS

- Who are your customers?
- Are they nearby or do you work with them through email, etc.?
- How many customers do you support?

Before Resume: WITHOUT THE FES INFORMATION

Administrative Assistant (40 hrs per wk) (Massachusetts Air National Guard) Jan 08 – Present. Provide administrative support to the Chief of Staff (Massachusetts Air National Guard). Provide reports to queries on personnel matters utilizing data systems RCAS and IPERMS. Track suspense's, Executive Summaries, correspondence, briefings, and investigations utilizing an electronic log system. Review Executive Summaries for content, format, and administrative errors. Maintain Payroll Worksheets for 35 personnel monitoring hours worked and vacations taken, and provide summary reports to supervisors and finance personnel. Manage Moral and Welfare fund requests for Massachusetts National Guard units by reviewing requests for legality, administrative correctness, submitting the paperwork to the State Military Department, and coordinating issuance of checks. Monitor the Chief of Staff's calendar for appointments and events. Assist in developing/ mentoring new personnel both enlisted and officer with office procedures.

After Resume: WITH THE FES INFORMATION

ADMINISTRATIVE ASSISTANT (40 hrs per wk) (Mass. Air National Guard)
Assistant to the Chief of Staff who oversees 3,000 Mass. National Guard Soldiers. Work independently to support all administrative, personnel, correspondence and payroll administration for the director.

COMPLEX ADMINISTRATION: Highly skilled in supporting multiple battalion deployments and re-integration and readiness during and following the ending of Iraq and Afghanistan. ACCOMPLISHMENT: Improved support for deployed and emergency support for the guardsmen. Organized and coordinated efficient ceremonies and events. Managed paperwork for complex deployments.

IMPLEMENT THE NATIONAL GUARD TECHNICIAN HANDBOOK. Implement and administer "The Technician Act of 1968", Public Law 90-486, for all support services for Reserves and Active duty personnel.

REPORTS AND DATABASE ADMINISTRATION AND COMPUTER SKILLS. Produce reports to queries on personnel matters utilizing data systems RCAS and IPERMS. Track suspenses, Executive Summaries, correspondence, briefings, and investigations utilizing an electronic log system.

CUSTOMER SERVICES FOR THE GUARD PERSONNEL: Manage Morale and Welfare fund requests for Massachusetts National Guard units by reviewing requests for legality and administrative correctness, submitting the paperwork to the State Military Department, and coordinating issuance of checks.

STEP 7

KSAs, Accomplishments, and Questionnaires

Have You Heard That KSAs Have Been Eliminated?

The traditional essays for the Knowledge, Skills, and Abilities (KSAs) narratives were eliminated. President Obama signed a memorandum to make immediate hiring reforms on May 11, 2010. See details at www.opm.gov/hiringreform/.

NOW THEY ARE EVERYWHERE!

KSAs are currently being covered in these sections of the federal application:

1. KSAs in the resume: work experience
2. KSAs in the resume: accomplishments
3. KSA in the Questionnaire: narrative questions
4. KSAs in the Questionnaire: multiple choice questions
5. KSAs as part of the Behavior-Based Interview

CCAR ACCOMPLISHMENT FORMAT | ^{STEP}7

The Office of Personnel Management has a recommended format for writing KSAs and your accomplishments record in a story-telling format: the Context, Challenge, Action, Result (CCAR) Model for writing better KSAs. This CCAR story-telling format is also great for the Behavior-Based Interview.

CONTEXT

The context should include the role you played in this example. Were you a team member, planner, organizer, facilitator, administrator, or coordinator? Also, include your job title at the time and the timeline of the project. You may want to note the name of the project or situation.

CHALLENGE

What was the specific problem that you faced that needed resolution? Describe the challenge of the situation. The problem could be disorganization in the office, new programs that needed to be implemented or supported, a change in management, a major project stalled, or a large conference or meeting being planned. The challenge can be difficult to write about. You can write the challenge last when you are drafting your KSAs.

ACTION

What did you do that made a difference? Did you change the way the office processed information, responded to customers, managed programs? What did you do?

RESULT

What difference did it make? Did this new action save dollars or time? Did it increase accountability and information? Did the team achieve its goals?

Use our free CCAR Accomplishment Builder!
www.resume-place.com/ccar_accomplishment

TEN RULES FOR WRITING KSAS OR ACCOMPLISHMENTS

 One excellent example per narrative will demonstrate that you have the knowledge, skills, and abilities for the position.

 If possible and appropriate, use a different example in each accomplishment statement.

 The typical length is 300 words or less.

4 Write your accomplishment examples with specific details, including the challenge of the example and the results.

5 Spell out ALL acronyms.

6 Write in the first person. "I serve as a point-of-contact for all inquiries that come to our office."

7 Quantify your results and accomplishments.

8 Draw material from all parts of your life, including community service, volunteer projects, or training.

9 Limit your paragraphs to 6 to 8 lines long for readability.

10 Proofread your writing again and again.

KSAs are now included in the federal resume and the Questionnaire with most applications. The Questionnaires are scored based on your answers, and the justification for your answers must be included in your resume.

Vacancy Announcement KSAs

Job Title: CONTRACT SPECIALIST
SERIES & GRADE: GS-1102-05/07

Knowledge, Skills and Abilities:
Possess at least one year of specialized experience performing work of the type listed in the following examples:

- developing, preparing, and presenting terms and conditions in bids or proposals related to the award of contracts;
- or negotiating and **awarding contracts, contract modifications**, and subcontract
- or in legal practice involving the analysis of procurement policies and procedures
- or administering the terms and conditions of contracts
- including such aspects as preparing contract modifications

KSAs Added into the Resume

Director of Logistics-Forward, Rank: Chief Warrant Officer 3
Camp Beuhring, Kuwait

CONTRACT AWARDS - REVIEWED SPECIFICATIONS AND STATEMENT OF WORK: Managed contracts valued at over $660 million. Developed, managed, and provided oversight for the logistical technical work specifications for 300 contractors work performance. Contracts included installation transportation support, field and sustainment maintenance, supply and services, multiclass SSA, retail fuel operations, life support, and food service operations for over 20,000 assigned personnel and over 80,000 US and Coalition Forces deployed to Kuwait, Afghanistan, Jordan, and Egypt.

ACCOMPLISHMENTS:

- Identified and processed for turn-in excess and obsolete equipment that totaled over $10 million for return to Sierra Army Depot saving the United States Army over $8 million in lost equipment.

- Maintained and accounted for over $70 million of Government Organizational Clothing & Individual Equipment (OCIE) in accordance with Army regulations, policies, guidelines, and procedures. Successfully conducted market research on Kuwait laundry service and local office supply stores. Determined which contracts offered best value for available funds.

CONTRACT MODIFICATIONS AND PROBLEM-SOLVING: Conducted an inventory of equipment valued at over $70 million. Recognized the need to modify the contract to manage the inventory management. Drafted the modification to request modified hours of the warehouse from 7 am to 7 pm to 7 pm to 7 am, so that we could perform the inventory at night rather than in the heat of the summer in over 120 degree weather. Successfully negotiated this modification.

KSAS IN THE RESUME: ACCOMPLISHMENTS

KSA: Ability to collect data and develop database reports

EMPLOYMENT SERVICES AND TRAINING COORDINATOR

02/2014 – Present
40 hours/week
Salary: $45,000

The Resume Place, Inc. Catonsville, MD
Supervisor: Kathryn Troutman, 410-744-4324, may contact

Key Accomplishment:

Supported the creation of a database that tracked the Ten Steps classes being taught worldwide by licensed trainers and the number of classes taught per base. Organized data from several Excel sheets and email records. Worked with a database programmer to create new app for an Adobe Quickbase Customer Relations Management System. Created new data to emphasize the importance of federal employment training for military spouses, transitioning military and civilians. Recognized that more than 226 military bases were licensed to teach Ten Steps to a Federal Job® in 2012; and more than 12,000 of the Ten Steps text–*Jobseeker's Guide*–were supporting the Ten Steps curriculum.

KSA: Ability to develop community readiness programs while building coalitions in the location community

FAMILY READINESS OFFICER (NF-0301-04)

11/2009 – 02/2013
40 hours/week
Salary: $45,000

Marine Corps Community Services, Camp Schwab, Okinawa, Japan
Supervisor: Taylor Sophreti, xxx-xxx-xxxx, may contact

Key Accomplishment:

As a Family Readiness Officer at Camp Schwab, Okinawa, Japan, it was my responsibility to coordinate efforts to celebrate the unit's children. Being overseas provided challenges to facilitating such celebrations, as resources were limited and expensive to obtain off-installation. During this time, tensions with the Okinawan populace were very high due to the planned relocation of a Marine Corps Air Station. Recognizing this tension, I suggested that the children of the local children's home and orphanage should be invited onto the base for fun activities with our unit's families. I contacted the camp's Community Liaison and Public Relations Specialist and worked through him to communicate our unit's intent with the leadership at the Nagomi Children's Home in Henoko. I also coordinated with the American Red Cross to collect items that would be useful to the children in the home, as well as blankets and toys. As a result of my efforts, seventeen children and five caregivers from the children's home participated in the event along with 28 American service and family members. This was the first unit-initiated event of its kind and the first real cultural exchange opportunity for many of the families in attendance.

Sometimes after you complete the typical multiple-choice Questionnaire, you might be asked to write narratives to support your Questionnaire answers.

Questionnaire with Narrative Responses (4,000 characters)

Grade - 09 Questions

Based on your responses to the previous questions in this vacancy announcement, you've been forwarded to this additional phase. The following question(s) relate to the questions asked previously in this announcement. You can review your responses by using the Previous button. To successfully complete your application, please review and follow these instructions:

1. Respond to each question. If you do not have related experience, enter "N/A".

2. Your responses to all of the questions in this announcement must be substantiated by the information in your resume.

3. Select the "Next" button at the bottom of each screen to make sure that you have viewed and responded to all questions.

4. If you wish to save your responses and come back later to complete your application, enter placeholder text in any empty text fields, and click the "Next" button. For each web page, the system will time out after one hour of inactivity and your entries will be lost unless you select the "Next" button.

5. You can return to the vacancy and complete your application, but all information must be submitted by the closing date of the announcement.

6. Once you have responded to all questions, select the "Finish" button. The system requires that you select the "FINISH" button, or your application will not be saved; your application will be incomplete, and you will not be considered for this vacancy.

7. After selecting "FINISH" you will be returned to the USAJOBS site.

* 1. Describe your experience evaluating policies/implementing programs related to operation /maintenance of commercial buildings/leased space; analyzing the effectiveness/efficiency of building operations, equipment & automated systems; interacting with customers/stakeholders regarding building services to assess needs/recommend solutions; analyzing real property budgetary/financial data. Limit your response to 4,000 characters, which is approximately one typewritten page.
Enter NA if Not Applicable.

4000 characters left (4000 character limit)

Job Title: Management and Program Analyst

Announcement Number: VX-15-FGa-1399830-BU   **USAJOBS Control Number:** 403835200

Applicant Name: KATHRYN K TROUTMAN

[Previous]   [Next]   [Save]

* Required information

Section 3   **Total Questions in this Assessment: 17**

The following statements pertain to your ability to analyze daily staffing trends, and collect data to determine effective application of policies and procedures.
For each task in the following group, choose the statement from the list below that best describes your experience and/or training. If applying by fax using OPM Form 1203-FX, darken the oval corresponding to that statement in Section 25. Please select only one letter for each item.

2. Work with supervisors to ensure employee adherence to schedules, schedules exception to daily routine, and report outcomes of any changes.

○ **A** I have not had education, training or experience in performing this task.

○ **B** I have had education or training in performing the task, but have not yet performed it on the job.

○ **C** I have performed this task on the job. My work on this task was monitored closely by a supervisor or senior employee to ensure compliance with proper procedures.

○ **D** I have performed this task as a regular part of a job. I have performed it independently and normally without review by a supervisor or senior employee.

⦿ **E** I am considered an expert in performing this task. I have supervised performance of this task or I am normally the person who is consulted by other workers to assist them in doing this task because of my expertise.

3. Administer requests for scheduling variations to account for staff meetings, special activities, etc.

○ **A** I have not had education, training or experience in performing this task.

○ **B** I have had education or training in performing the task, but have not yet performed it on the job.

○ **C** I have performed this task on the job. My work on this task was monitored closely by a supervisor or senior employee to ensure compliance with proper procedures.

○ **D** I have performed this task as a regular part of a job. I have performed it independently and normally without review by a supervisor or senior employee.

⦿ **E** I am considered an expert in performing this task. I have supervised performance of this task or I am normally the person who is consulted by other workers to assist them in doing this task because of my expertise.

4. Keep abreast of changes occurring in programs that may affect the volume, quality or type of data collected, and make recommendations to ensure adherence to overall objectives.

○ **A** I have not had education, training or experience in performing this task.

○ **B** I have had education or training in performing the task, but have not yet performed it on the job.

○ **C** I have performed this task on the job. My work on this task was monitored closely by a supervisor or senior employee to ensure compliance with proper procedures.

○ **D** I have performed this task as a regular part of a job. I have performed it independently and normally without review by a supervisor or senior employee.

⦿ **E** I am considered an expert in performing this task. I have supervised performance of this task or I am normally the person who is consulted by other workers to assist them in doing this task because of my expertise.

KSAS AS PART OF THE BEHAVIOR-BASED INTERVIEW

Prepare five CCAR accomplishment stories prepared in advance to talk about at the interview. Use our free CCAR Builder to write your accomplishment stories: www.resume-place.com/ccar-accomplishment

Bill Nethers' CCAR Interview Accomplishment Story for Contract Specialist Application - HIRED

Title of Your Story
Successfully Negotiated and Purchased Army Blues Band New Instruments from Small Retail Business.

Context
I was the Reserves Army Band Leader for the Army National Guard in Baltimore, and in my civilian job I was the Department Manager at Appalachian Blue Grass. I had recently stood up the new Blues Band in order to maintain our musicians, the quality of our performances, and morale of our Soldiers.

Challenge
The challenge was budget for purchasing instruments for the new Blues Band. We needed to purchase the items with a very tight budget, and I was very familiar with this product line. I needed to purchase 16 instruments with a total budget of up to $50K. I wanted to position our small town music shop as the Most Favored Customer for the U.S. Army Band. It was challenging to work with the owner of the small business to negotiate and work with government contracts for instrument products.

Actions

1. I researched quality products and negotiated the best prices and availability from vendors and manufacturers through my role as Department Manager.

2. I utilized my knowledge of the manufacturers and products in order to build the best instrument inventory possible for the new Blues Band.

3. I worked with a Contract Specialist with the U.S. Army to prepare the contracts and manage the competitive bidding for our specialty acoustical instruments.

Results
We successfully purchased $49K in acoustical guitars and electric equipment in just 120 days from a small business for our first Blues Band concert in Camp Liberty, Baghdad. The concert was attended by more than 3,000 civilians and military personnel. Morale was fantastic and it was a great accomplishment for me in that I established the Blues Band and I managed the contracting of the instruments for our expert musicians. The Blues Band is one of the featured bands for the U.S. Army "Pershing's Own" Bands. I successfully managed the purchase of high quality acoustical guitars, banjos, dobros and electric instruments for a new Blues Band and other band features with the small retail business, which became a Small Set-Aside Business / GSA contractor and vendor for the U.S. Army Bands.

Cover letters are usual optional. Read the vacancy announcement instructions!

To write a great cover letter, go to:
www.resume-place.com/resources/cover-letter-builder/

Specialized Experience
Add a list of skills and experience that you can offer that matches the specialized experience in the announcement.

Compelling
Tell the reader why you are an excellent candidate and you believe in their mission.

Passion and Interest in the Mission
Write about your interest in the mission of the agency or organization. If you know the mission and can speak about it in a sentence, you can stand out above your competition.

Letter of Interest
The cover letter IS a letter of interest. You are interested in the job. The cover letter is more than a transmittal. Take this opportunity to sell your special qualifications, certifications, training, and mission-related experiences. This is another small writing test.

Adding or Uploading a Short Cover Letter into the Resume Builder
With USAJOBS, you can add the letter into Additional Information section. With Application Manager, you can upload your cover letter.

Special Considerations
You can mention your willingness to relocate, eligibility for non-competitive spouse appointments, veterans' preference, reasons for wanting to move, such as family, and other special interest items in the cover letter.

Why Hire Me?
Be sure to mention your best qualities (that match the announcement).

Cover letters for federal jobs are usually NOT required, but you can send a cover letter along with your federal resume for the supervisor, if your resume is referred to a supervisor. Be sure to include: your specialized experience related to the position; significant education or training; and a top accomplishment that can be impressive. Add details about your job search, such as your interest in a specific geographic area. Include a sentence about your interest in the mission of the agency.

This sample was created using our Cover Letter Builder: www.resume-place.com/resources/cover-letter-builder/

JOHN SMITH
1000 Smith Avenue | Ft. McCoy, WI 90210
444-444-4444 | john.smith@netflix.com

June 5, 2015

Department Name
Division Name
Address Line 1
Address Line 2

RE: USAJOBS Announcement #: XXX-XXXX-XXX

To Whom It May Concern:
Please accept my resume and supporting materials in application for the Geospatial Analyst position with National Geospatial Intelligence Agency (NGA) (USAJOBS Announcement #: XXX-XXXX-XXX).
My relevant experience for the position includes:

- Three years of experience in military geospatial intelligence environments with in-depth experience in map design, map production, and geospatial intelligence support.
- I have collaborated with entities such as U.S. Central Command, U.S. Cyber Command, and the Intelligence Community.
- I am a subject matter expert in cartography, including 3D modeling, and am fluent in the use of geospatial analysis and mapping software.

I believe that I would be an asset to your organization because:

- I have delivered high-quality geospatial support for several agencies within the Intelligence Community. I possess overseas military experience, including in support of active combat operations in the Middle East.
- My military record demonstrates that I am a skilled analyst and briefer with substantial real-world experience. I am known for my ability to communicate, to pull long hours, and for my precision in overseeing collection and mapping efforts.
- I am committed to providing rapid analyses and quality recommendations regardless of situational complexity. I will bring those skill sets and problem solving qualities to bear on NGA's challenges.

Thank you for your time and consideration. I look forward to your response.

Sincerely,
John Smith

Enclosures: Resume, DD-214

STEP

Apply for Jobs with USAJOBS

USAJOBS is the website you will use to apply for federal jobs: www.usajobs.gov

BASIC STEPS

PART 1: GET READY ON USAJOBS
- Set up your login
- Set up your profile
- Select an announcement to apply for
- Upload your resume or use the Resume Builder
- Upload documents

PART 2: APPLY FOR JOBS
- Complete the Questionnaire (on a different site)
- SUBMIT!

BE SURE TO APPLY AHEAD OF THE DEADLINE!

Getting Started with USAJOBS

Use this getting started guide to set up your USAJOBS account and apply for federal jobs!

1. Logging In: Write Down Your Password!

Applicants routinely complain that they forget their password, which must include numbers, symbols, and letters. Make sure you link your account to a personal email, not a work email, so that you can access it at home.

2. Edit Your Profile: Answer Carefully!

The profile section of USAJOBS will pop up when you register or can be accessed by clicking on "Edit Profile" on the Main page. You will be asked to enter Contact Information, Hiring Eligibility, Preferences, Demographic Information, and Account Information.

> Your SSN will not be required in USAJOBS. But you might have to add your SSN and DOB into the questionnaire application system.

My Account

Profile

Resumes

Saved Searches

Inbox (3)

Saved Jobs

Saved Documents

Application Status

☑ Contact Information ☑ Hiring Eligibility ☑ Other ☑ Demographic ☑ Account Information

Please Note: Fields with an (*) are **required fields.**

Legal Name ⚙

Prefix	First Name *	Middle Name	Last Name *	Suffix
--Select--	KATHRYN	K	TROUTMAN	--Select--

Address ⚙

Address 1 *   655 West Lake Road

Address 2

Country *   United States

Postal Code *	City/Town *	State/Territory/Province *
21228	Catonsville	Maryland

Telephone ⚙

Telephone 1 *   Day Phone   907-333-3333   Ext:

Telephone 2   --Select--   Ext:

Telephone 3   --Select--   Ext:

Email

Primary Email Address *   kathryn@resume-place.com

Secondary Email Address

What is my Secondary Email Address used for?

What is your email format preference? ⚙ ⦿ HTML ◯ Text
Some email providers block HTML messages. Select "Text" to ensure your emails go through.

Be advised that only one account can be created for each email address. Be sure the email account you use is only accessible by you and the email account is properly secured.

Cancel   Save   Next

GET READY ON USAJOBS CONT.

3. Contact Information

Be sure to enter an email address for your home, not work. In the event that you forget your password, the system may need to contact you via email for confirmation. You want to make sure you have listed an email address that you can always access.

Email

Primary Email Address * `kathryn@resume-place.com`

Secondary Email Address [　　　　　　　　　　]
What is my Secondary Email Address used for?

What is your email format preference? ❓ ● HTML ○ Text
Some email providers block HTML messages. Select "Text" to ensure your emails go through.

Be advised that only one account can be created for each email address. Be sure the email account you use is only accessible by you and the email account is properly secured.

---

4. Eligibility

Your answers to these questions can determine whether or not your resume and application ever make it to Human Resources. So, answer carefully.

U.S. Citizen: Most federal jobs require citizenship.

Selective Service: If you are a man, did you sign up for the draft? Many times you may not remember doing so, but it is a normal part of getting a driver's license, voting, etc.

Contractors do not have "reinstatement eligibility."

Current and Former Federal Employees: Select the appropriate answer regarding federal employment status and reinstatement eligibility. Also answer questions about your agency, organization, pay plan, series, and grade level/pay.

---

4. Please select the statement below which best reflects your federal employment status (if applicable). * ❓

○ I am not and have never been a federal civilian employee.

● I am currently a federal civilian employee.

○ I am a former federal civilian employee with reinstatement eligibility.

○ I am a former federal civilian employee but do not have reinstatement eligibility.

- **By which Federal agency and organization are you currently employed?**

  Select Department: [Department Of Homeland Security ▼]

  Select Agency: [Transportation Security Administration ▼]

- **Indicate the pay plan, series, grade level/pay band of the highest permanent graded position you ever held as a Federal Civilian Employee. (Question does not apply to members of the armed forces covered under Title 10.)**

  Pay Plan: [GS – General Schedule ▼]

  Occupational Series: [0342 Support Services Administration ▼]

  Highest Pay Grade: [09]

5. Eligibility Documentation

Veterans

When claiming preference, veterans must provide a copy of their DD-214, Certificate of Release or Discharge from Active Duty, or other acceptable documentation.

Applicants claiming 10 point preference will need to submit Form SF-15, Application for 10-point veterans' preference. Ensure your documentation reflects the character of discharge.

If you do not upload your documentation, you will not be eligible for veterans' preference.

Federal Employees

If you are a current federal employee, you must upload your SF-50, or you will not be considered for jobs open only to current feds.

Sometimes they will ask for your last year's evaluation. Make sure it is signed.

Veterans' Document Upload:

When claiming veterans' preference, preference eligibles must provide a copy of their DD 214, Certificate of Release or Discharge from Active Duty, or other acceptable documentation. Applicants claiming 10 point preference will need to submit an SF-15, Application for 10-point Veterans' Preference.

For current service members who have not yet been discharged, a certification letter of expected discharge or release from active duty within 120 days under honorable conditions is required at the time of application. Ensure your documentation reflects the character of discharge.

Document Title: [   ]

Document Type: ❓ Select Document:
[DD-214 ▼] [Choose File] No file chosen

Files must be less than 3mb and can be in one of the following formats: GIF, JPG, JPEG, PNG, RTF, PDF, or Word (DOC or DOCX).

[Upload] [Cancel]

GET READY ON USAJOBS CONT.

6. Veterans' Preference

Veterans can select the preference type that applies to them. Veterans' preference may also apply to spouses, widows, and parents in some situations. If you think you will receive a disability rating, but have not received it yet, you must wait before selecting the 10 point category. You will need to provide paperwork to prove any disability rating. To determine your points, you can use this automated advisory system from the Department of Labor: http://www.dol.gov/elaws/vetspref.htm.

Even if you are not eligible for preference, as a veteran you may be eligible for other types of special hiring authorities if you served at least three years and received an honorable discharge.

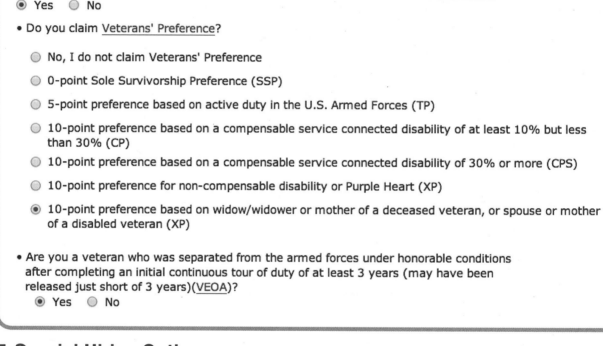

3. Are you a Veteran of the U.S. Armed Forces or are you eligible for "derived" preference? *
   ◉ Yes ○ No

   • Do you claim Veterans' Preference?

   ○ No, I do not claim Veterans' Preference

   ○ 0-point Sole Survivorship Preference (SSP)

   ○ 5-point preference based on active duty in the U.S. Armed Forces (TP)

   ○ 10-point preference based on a compensable service connected disability of at least 10% but less than 30% (CP)

   ○ 10-point preference based on a compensable service connected disability of 30% or more (CPS)

   ○ 10-point preference for non-compensable disability or Purple Heart (XP)

   ◉ 10-point preference based on widow/widower or mother of a deceased veteran, or spouse or mother of a disabled veteran (XP)

   • Are you a veteran who was separated from the armed forces under honorable conditions after completing an initial continuous tour of duty of at least 3 years (may have been released just short of 3 years)(VEOA)?
   ◉ Yes ○ No

7. Special Hiring Options

There are many government initiatives that give employment preference to specific and targeted segments of the population. The special hiring options include:

Veterans Recruitment Appointment (VRA): An excepted authority that allows agencies to appoint eligible veterans without competition if the veteran has received a campaign badge for service during a war or in a campaign or expedition; or is a disabled veteran; or has received an Armed Forces Service Medal for participation in a military operation; or is a recently separated veteran (within the last three years) and separated under honorable conditions. Appointments under this authority may be made at any grade level up to and including GS-11 or equivalent. This is an excepted service appointment, which can be converted to competitive service after two years.

30% or More Disabled Veteran: A person who was separated under honorable conditions from active duty in the Armed Forces performed at any time and who has established the present existence of a service-connected disability rated at 30% or greater or is receiving compensation, disability retirement benefits, or pension because of a public statute administered by the Department of Veterans Affairs or a military department.

Disabled veterans who have completed a VA training program: A person who meets the definition of a disabled veteran and has successfully completed a program to receive training or work experience at VA.

Military Spouse: Military spouses are eligible under this authority if the active duty military spouse: 1) receives a Permanent Change of Station (PCS) move; 2) has a 100% disability rating; or 3) died while on active duty. Each of these categories has different eligibility criteria that must be met.

Certain Former Overseas Employees: A family member (which includes same-sex domestic partners) of a federal civilian employee or military member who has completed 52 weeks of service in a federal position overseas is eligible for appointment in the competitive service for a period of three years following the date of their return to the United States from the overseas area.

Schedule A Disabled Individuals with Intellectual Disabilities, Severe Physical Disabilities, or Psychiatric Disabilities may apply for non-competitive appointment through the Schedule A (5 C.F.R. 213.3102(u)) hiring authority. Documentation of the disability is required from a licensed medical professional; a licensed vocational rehabilitation specialist; or any federal, state, or District of Columbia agency or U.S. territory that issues or provides disability benefits.

VETERANS WHO ARE DISABLED SHOULD SELECT "SCHEDULE A DISABLED" IN ADDITION TO THEIR HIRING PREFERENCE IN QUESTION 4.

Special Hiring Options ❓

Select from among the special hiring authorities listed below for which you are eligible. (Please note that agencies will require documentation of eligibility prior to your appointment.)

Identification of eligibility for any special hiring authority is entirely voluntary, and you will not be subject to any adverse treatment if you decline to provide it. If you do not wish to volunteer this information at this time, you may still choose to apply for jobs, as they are announced, under any of these special hiring authorities for which you are eligible. If you volunteer to provide information here about the special hiring authorities for which you believe you are eligible, then agencies who are searching for potential applicants to hire under one of these authorities may be able to locate your resume through USAJOBS and invite you to apply. Otherwise, this information will be retained in the USAJOBS database and not disclosed. For information on each of the special hiring options below, please review the definitions on our Special Hiring Options page.

- ☑ Veterans Recruitment Appointment (VRA)
- ☑ 30% or More Disabled Veteran
- ☑ Disabled veterans who have completed a VA training program
- ☑ Military Spouse
- ☐ Certain former overseas employees
- ☑ Schedule A Disabled

Cancel | Previous | Save | Next

---

8. Other - Important Questions!

Applicants should choose carefully in this section because their answers will determine whether they are eligible later.

Are you willing to travel? If you say "No" you will be disqualified from a job, even if the amount of travel is very minimal. Be sure that you can travel at least 25% in case you must attend a conference.

What type of work are you willing to accept? Consider that more federal agencies are using "temp" and "term" jobs to fill positions when money is tight, or when the future is unknown. For example, many jobs that came out of the mortgage crisis were initially term jobs that eventually may become permanent.

If you accidentally apply for a "temp" or "term" job, but didn't click the button on this page, your application won't be read at all by Human Resources.

What type of work schedule are you willing to accept? Consider being flexible.

Select your desired work location(s). Select all of U.S. and if you apply for a job abroad, remember to come back and select that location as well.

If you only pick D.C., you might later be disqualified for a job in Baltimore.

9. Demographic

Your answers to this question are voluntary and do not affect whether or not you will be hired.

10. Personal Information

Write down your password! Also, you can choose to receive "Notification Alerts" on your application. This is important in case a job posting is pulled or re-announced.

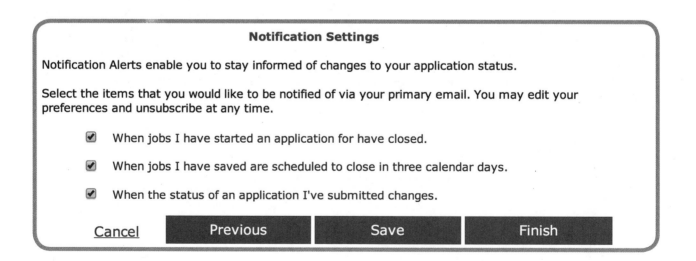

Notification Settings

Notification Alerts enable you to stay informed of changes to your application status.

Select the items that you would like to be notified of via your primary email. You may edit your preferences and unsubscribe at any time.

☑ When jobs I have started an application for have closed.

☑ When jobs I have saved are scheduled to close in three calendar days.

☑ When the status of an application I've submitted changes.

| Cancel | Previous | Save | Finish |

11. My Account Main Page

- **Profile:** Personal Information, Hiring Eligibility, Preferences, Demographic Information, and Account Information

- **Resumes:** You can save up to five resumes in USAJOBS. That includes uploaded resumes and resumes built using the USAJOBS Resume Builder.

- **Saved Searches:** Save your preferences for jobs you've searched in the past.

- **Saved Jobs:** You can bookmark jobs you like.

- **Saved Documents:** Your uploaded documents appear here. If you are using education to qualify for experience, you must upload your transcripts. They can be unofficial (HR will ask for official transcripts if you are hired).

- **Application Status:** This section helps you track and follow up on your application and determine if you've actually applied.

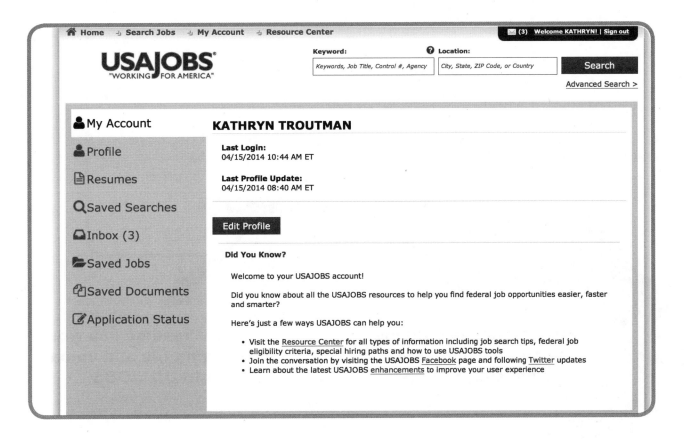

USAJOBS RESUME BUILDER VS. UPLOAD

Using the USAJOBS Resume Builder increases the chances that you will apply correctly for a federal job. If you upload a federal resume into USAJOBS, make sure you include all of the details that are marked as "required" in the USAJOBS Resume Builder, such as the month and year for employment start and end dates.

Store up to five resumes in USAJOBS.

Resume 1: MSW Veterans Administrati...
View | Edit | Duplicate | Delete

Status: Not Searchable
Make Searchable

Format: USAJOBS Resume
Source: Built with USAJOBS Resume Builder

Resume 2: IT Spec, Customer Service...
View | Edit | Duplicate | Delete

Status: Not Searchable
Make Searchable

Format: USAJOBS Resume
Source: Built with USAJOBS Resume Builder

Resume 3: IT Specialist Veteran JS ...
View | Edit | Duplicate | Delete

Status: Not Searchable
Make Searchable

Format: USAJOBS Resume
Source: Built with USAJOBS Resume Builder

Resume 4: Air Traffic Controller (T...
View | Edit | Duplicate | Delete

Status: Not Searchable
Make Searchable

Format: USAJOBS Resume
Source: Built with USAJOBS Resume Builder

[Build New Resume] [Upload New Resume]

You have created **4** of **5** possible resumes. You are able to upload and store **5** resumes to your My USAJOBS account.

Use the Resume Builder to create your resume from start to finish

Create a resume in a word processing file and upload into USAJOBS

Application Manager, an automated system run by USA Staffing, is frequently used in conjunction with USAJOBS, where Application Manager is the utility for administering the self-assessment and supplemental data questions. Application Manager is now run in conjunction with USAJOBS so that it is no longer necessary to have a separate Application Manager account.

When you select Apply Now on USAJOBS, you will then choose the resume to take with you to Application Manager.

Resume - Select one of your stored USAJOBS resumes to send :
- ○ MSW Veterans Administration
- ○ IT Spec, Customer Service, GS-2210-11
- ○ IT Specialist Veteran JS Guide 5th
- ○ Air Traffic Controller (Trainee)
- ○ Resume for CDP

Attachment(s) - Select one or more of your Saved Documents to send (or first <u>Save Job and Upload Documents</u>). :
- ☐ COVER (Class Notes Fedres Writing)
- ☐ COVER (ED Cover Letter)

Fields below with an asterisks (*) are required.

* ☐ I have <u>previewed my resume</u> . The selected document includes the information I wish to provide with this application.

☐ Allow me to attach demographic information to the application. <u>Review or update your demographic information.</u>

* ☐ I certify, to the best of my knowledge and belief, all the information submitted by me with my application for employment is true, complete, and made in good faith, and that I have truthfully and accurately represented my work experience, knowledge, skills, abilities and education (degrees, accomplishments, etc.). I understand that the information provided may be investigated. I understand that misrepresenting my experience or education, or providing false or fraudulent information in or with my application may be grounds for not hiring me or for firing me after I begin work. I also understand that false or fraudulent statements may be punishable by fine or imprisonment (18 U.S.C. 1001).

| Apply for this position now! | Cancel |

If the agency is using Application Manager as the Automated Recruitment System for their questionnaire and document collection, you will be taken to this site automatically from USAJOBS.

Ready to Submit?

Submit My Answers

1. You can utilize the USAJOBS resume or upload another resume and other pertinent application documents, as well as other information that they might request, i.e. your last evaluation, DD-214 (veterans), and transcripts.

2. You will complete the Self-Assessment Questions. Follow all steps through "SUBMIT MY ANSWERS," or your application will not be submitted.

AUTOMATED RECRUITMENT SYSTEMS (ARS)

Each agency can select an Automated Recruitment System (ARS) for managing and tracking applicants.

The applicant Questionnaires are basically similar among the different systems and will usually include multiple choice and self-assessment style questions.

Carefully follow the directions!

See examples of different automated recruitment systems on these two pages.

Monster.com (Transportation Security Administration)

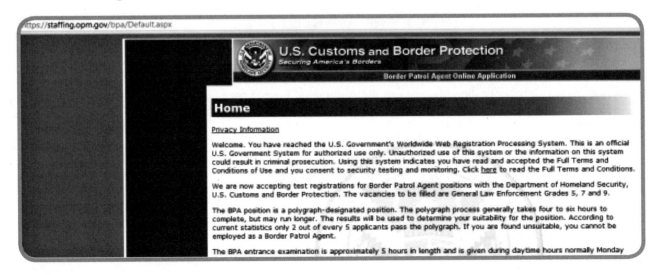

USAStaffing (U.S. Customs and Border Protection)

You may be required to take an additional Occupational Assessment as part of your application. This exam is a new feature that we have started seeing with a small number of applications. It is essentially an online test which may include these following areas: Math, Judgment, Reasoning, Interaction, and Reading.

The test will take around 1.5 to 3 hours to complete, and you will have to complete the assessment within a certain time frame, but you do not have to complete the assessment in a single sitting.

Be sure to read the computer system requirements carefully before starting the exam.

Read more: https://usahire.opm.gov/assess/default/sample/Sample.action

USA Hire℠
Transforming Government One Hire At A Time

Assessments and Sample Questions

When applying for this position, you will be asked to complete several of the assessments listed below. A summary of each assessment is provided as is a sample question. The specific assessments you will be asked to take will differ depending on the job to which you are applying. None of the answers you select below will actually be submitted. This page is only provided as an example of the look and feel of the actual assessments.

Occupational Math Assessment

In this assessment, you will be presented with multiple-choice questions that measure your arithmetic and mathematical reasoning skills. You will be asked to solve word problems and perform numerical calculations. You will also be asked to work with percentages, fractions, decimals, proportions, basic algebra, basic geometry, and basic probability.

All of the information you need to answer the questions is provided in the question text. Knowledge of Federal rules, regulations, or policies is NOT required to answer the questions.

You MAY use a calculator and scratch paper to answer the questions.

Read the questions carefully and choose the **best answer** for each question. Once you have selected your response, click on the RECORD ANSWER button. **You will not be able to review/change your answers once you have submitted them.**

This assessment contains several questions. For each question, you will have **5 minutes** to select your answer.

A sample question is shown below.

Occupational Math Example	4 Min. 28 Sec. Remaining

Question Solve for x.

$$3x - 3 = 6$$

○ 1
○ 3
○ 6
○ 9
○ 12

STEP 9

Track and Follow Up on Your Applications

You can find out what happened to your applications! Learn to track and follow up with HR and your USAJOBS account.

How Long Does It Take to Fill a Federal Job?

The current goal for length of time to fill a federal vacancy is 45 days from the date of posting job announcement. However, in our experience, the curent average time seems to be more around the range of 90 to 120 days.

How People Are Hired: The Competitive Process

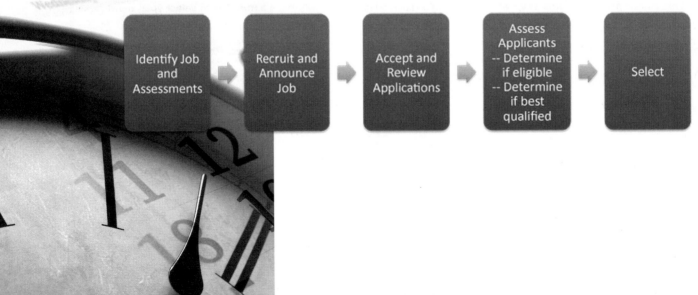

Identify Job and Assessments → Recruit and Announce Job → Accept and Review Applications → Assess Applicants -- Determine if eligible -- Determine if best qualified → Select

FOLLOW-UP TECHNIQUES |

USAJOBS & Application Manager

Most automated application systems have tracking systems to check the status of your application. Be sure to check your status regularly. Save your user name and password for each builder.

Find Out Your Application Score Online

You can check on the status of your applications in both USAJOBS and Application Manager. The Notice of Results (NOR) will tell you the outcome of your application.

When to Call HR

You can call HR to find out what happened to your application if you haven't heard anything two to three weeks past the closing date. Many HR specialists respond to phone messages.

Sample Telephone Message Script

"Hello, I'm Kathryn Troutman. I'm calling regarding my application submitted for announcement number 10505 for Writer-Editor, GS-12. The closing date was 3/31 and I'm checking on the status of the recruitment. I can be reached at 410-744-4324 from 9 until 5, Monday through Friday, Eastern Standard Time. If you get voicemail, you can leave a message regarding the position. Thank you for your time. I look forward to your information."

Emails from Human Resources

If you receive an email from the HR specialist concerning your qualifications for the position and you can't understand the email, just write back or call to get clarification of the email.

Emailing the HR Representative

If there is an email address on the announcement, you could try contacting the Human Resources specialist by email. You can contact the HR specialist to check on the status of your applications and find out your application score if this information is not posted online. Here is a sample letter:

Subject line: Status of announcement 10101

Dear Ms. Jones,

I submitted my Federal resume, KSAs, and evaluation for the position of Writer-Editor, announcement no. 10101 on Dec. 22 by USPS. I'd like to check the status of my application and the recruitment, please.

Is it still open and was I found qualified? Thank you very much for your time.

Sincerely,

Kathryn Troutman

Daytime phone: 410-744-4324 (M-F EST) messages okay

Application Package Status: See Details Tab

Job Title: INVENTORY MANAGEMENT SPECIALIST

Vacancy Identification Number: 1026916

Announcement Number: 9S-TRANS-1026916-038368-MAF

USAJOBS Control Number: 358913500

Applicant: KATHRYN K TROUTMAN

Closing Date: Thursday, January 16, 2014

Contact: AFPC RSC - (800)525-0102

[Change My Answers] [Add Documents] [Update Biographic Information] [View/Print My Answers]

Most information below pertains to the most recent version of your Application Package. (Explain This.)

Notice to Applicants: Please ensure you keep copies of all documents you uploaded or faxed, including your resume, as well as any notifications sent to you. They will be deleted from the system after 3 years of the closing date of the announcement.

| Details | Checklist |

Assessments

Status	Name	Date Submitted	Due Date
Complete	Assessment Questionnaire	1/16/2014 2:36:29 PM	
Complete	Assessment Questionnaire	1/16/2014 2:36:29 PM	

Documents

* Security Alert: Protect your privacy

	Status	Document Type	Source	Re-Use Document	Date Received	Original File Name
View	Processed	Resume	USAJOBS		01/16/2014 02:31 PM	
	Not Received	Cover Letter				
	Not Received	DD-214				
	Not Received	Other				
	Not Received	Other Veterans Document				

Messages

	Message Type	Date Emailed	Date Printed
View	Notice of Results (NORs)	1/18/2014 1:27:48 AM	
View	Notification Letter	1/21/2014 4:12:24 PM	
View	Acknowledgement Letter	1/16/2014 2:36:29 PM	

Application Processing Status

Status	Date Submitted

Notice of Results (NOR) gives you information about the status of your application. The types of responses could be: Not Eligible, Eligible, Best Qualified, Best Qualified and Not Among the Most Qualified to be Referred, Best Qualified and Referred. It's important to check your NORs, so that you can gauge the success of your applications.

You can find your Notice of Results in Applicationmanager.gov under My Application Packages. You may also receive your results by email, or you may contact the HR representative listed in the announcement to find out what happened with your application.

Jobseeker wrote EMAIL TO HR | RESULT: REFERRED (Good News!)

EMAIL TO HR:
To: Work4Us
Subject: USAJOBS Vacancy ID: 1280066
Announcement: 15-063-SWA-DE
USAJOBS Control Number: 389718200

Dear Human Resource Manager,
Good morning and happy Martin Luther King, Jr. Day. My name is Mariano and I am contacting you to request a day and time for an interview this week. I hope this request is not taken negatively, but would sincerely like to meet with the hiring authority so that we may engage in a dialogue concerning my experience, appearance, and history. I thank you for the time you have taken to read my email and look forward to your reply soon.
Sincerely, Mariano

THE ANSWER FROM HR:
Mariano, **Your application was forwarded on to the selecting official for further consideration.** Once the selecting official receives the applications they may choose to interview all, some or none of the applicants. They are able to choose from those applicants who they would like to select for the position. They will contact you directly if an interview is desired. Please let us know if you have any further concerns.

AUTOMATED EMAIL FROM HR | RESULT: EL (Eligible) for GS-05/07

From: usastaffingoffice@opm.gov
Subject: Notice of Results (NORs) Vacancy ID: 1315752

This is a record of your application for Federal Employment in the occupation shown below. This is not a job offer. This notice provides information contained in your record as it appears in the files of the Servicing Office shown above. Your qualification and any veteran preference claims are subject to verification.

Series - PositionTitle: 1102 - CONTRACT SPECIALIST
You must meet all medical, suitability, and qualification requirements to be considered for a position.
Spec Code: Spec Title: Grade: Rating:
001 Contract Specialist 05 EL
001 Contract Specialist 07 EL

NOTICE OF RESULTS (NOR) CONT.

Automated Email from HR | RESULT: Score of 70 (Not Great News)

NOTICE OF RESULTS

This notification refers to the application you recently submitted to this office for the position shown below:

Thank you for applying for a Senior Executive Services (SES) position with U.S. Immigration and Customs Enforcement (ICE). **You have been found qualified for this position.**

You will receive separate email notification indicating whether you will be further considered in the selection process.

Series - PositionTitle: 1811 - Special Agent in Charge-2015
Spec Code: Spec Title: Grade: Rating:

   002   Special Agent In Charge 00   70

Automated Email from HR | RESULT: EL (Eligible) and Not Referred

HHS CMS CENTER
This refers to the application you recently submitted to this office for the position below:
Position Title: Health Insurance Specialist
Series/Grade: 0107-13
Hiring Office: Center for Medicaid and CHIP Services CMCS
Spec Title: Health Insurance Specialist
Grade: 13
Rating: EL

Referral Type: Open to all qualified candidates
Referral Name: AJU-14-MSt-02039S0
Status: NR - Not Referred

Status Code: Status Message:
NR - Not   We have reviewed your application and found you eligible for the position listed above
Referred   Status code. However, you were not among the most highly qualified candidates. Therefore, your name will not be referred to the employing agency at this time.
Rating Code: Rating Message:
EL   You are eligible for this specialty and grade.

This email is to extend a conditional offer of employment to you.

Email from HR | RESULT: Conditional Offer of Employment!

Subject: Tentative Selection Notification: CBP Technician, GS-1802-05, Eastport ID

Good afternoon _____,
This email is to extend a conditional offer of employment to you for the following position:

Job Title: CBP Technician
Payplan/Job Series/Grade/Step: GS-1802-05 Step 01
Full Performance Level: GS-07
Appointing Authority: Schedule A: This is a non-competitive appointment in the excepted service. You may be non-competitively converted to a career or career-conditional appointment in the competitive service after completing 2 years of satisfactory service under this authority. Conversion is at managements' discretion.

Please reply to the above address no later than close of business on Monday, April 13, 2015 as to whether you wish to accept this offer.

We are making this conditional offer of employment based on a projection of hiring needs, the existence of a vacant funded position, the absence of any hiring restrictions, and any other controlling factors.

Automated Email from HR | RESULT: HIRED! (Congratulations!)

Avue
TECHNOLOGIES CORPORATION

Congratulations! You have been hired!

Court Services and Offender Supervision Agency
Drug Testing Clerk (OA), GL-0102-04
Announcement Number: CSS-14-102-DEU-CP
WASHINGTON, Dist of Columbia

Congratulations! You have been selected for this position. We will be in touch with you very soon to answer your questions and to discuss the details of your coming to work for Court Services and Offender Supervision Agency. If you need assistance concerning a particular vacancy, please refer to the vacancy announcement and contact the person named there. If you need technical assistance please log in and consult the Avue Dojo using our chat feature. Thank you for your interest in this vacancy. This email is for informational purposes only, please do not reply to this email.

STEP 10

Interview for a Federal Job

The federal job interview is a TEST. Your answers will be graded.

You need to practice, research, and prepare for it to be successful. To stand and out above the competition, be prepared to talk about your relevant skills and experiences. Impress the hiring team that YOU CAN DO THE JOB being offered. Demonstrate confidence, interest, and enthusiasm.

THE PERFORMANCE-BASED INTERVIEW IS A TEST: BE PREPARED!

Be prepared for a new interview format, the Performance-Based Interview. Be prepared to give examples in answers to seven to ten questions that will be situation or experience based. If you have an example of how you led a team, provided training, or managed a project, be prepared to talk about the project and teamwork. The best answers will be examples that demonstrate your past performance.

Know the paperwork

Know the vacancy announcement, agency mission, and office function. Read your resume and KSAs out loud with enthusiasm. Become convinced that you are very well qualified for the job and that the agency NEEDS you to help achieve their mission.

Do the necessary research

Go online to research the agency, department, and position. Read press releases about the organization. Go to www.washingtonpost.com and search for the organization to see if there are any recent news events.

Confidence, Knowledge, and Skills

In order to "sell" yourself for a new position, you have to believe in your abilities. Read books and listen to tapes that will help boost your confidence and give you the support you need to "brag" on your work skills. Don't forget or be afraid to use "I"!

Practice

In front of a mirror, tape recorder, video camera, family member, friend, anyone who volunteers to listen to you.

TYPES OF FEDERAL INTERVIEWS

Telephone Interview

Prepare as though you are meeting the person in an office. Get dressed nicely, have your papers neatly organized, create a quiet environment, and project a focused listening and communications style. If you are great on the phone, you can get a second interview.

Individual Interview

For the one-on-one interview, get ready for an unknown Q&A format. Prepare your questions and answers ahead of time and be ready. Be friendly, professional, and answer the questions. Practice for this interview.

Group/Panel Interview

Two to six professional staff will interview and observe your answers. This is a difficult interview format, but it is not used too often. Just look at the person asking the question while he or she is speaking. Answer the question by looking at the person asking, but look around the room as well.

Tell Me About Yourself

Write a three-minute introduction that you could use in an interview. It should include information relevant to the position.

A Significant Accomplishment

Write one significant accomplishment that you will describe in an interview.

Select Your Best Competencies

Make a list of your best core competencies.

Write Your Most Critical Skills

Make a list of your best skills that will be most marketable to this employer.

TYPICAL PERFORMANCE-BASED INTERVIEW QUESTIONS

Typical interview questions will be:

Job-Related
Open-Ended
Behavior-Based
Skill- and Competency-Based

Competency-Based Sample Interview Questions

Often, an interviewer will ask questions that directly relate to a competency required for the position. Here are some examples.

Attention to Detail: Describe a project you were working on that required attention to detail.

Communication: Describe a time when you had to communicate under difficult circumstances.

Conflict Management: Describe a situation where you found yourself working with someone who didn't like you. How did you handle it?

Continuous Learning: Describe a time when you recognized a problem as an opportunity.

Customer Service: Describe a situation in which you demonstrated an effective customer service skill.

Decisiveness: Tell me about a time when you had to stand up for a decision you made even though it made you unpopular.

Leadership: Describe a time when you exhibited participatory management.

Planning, Organizing, Goal Setting: Describe a time when you had to complete multiple tasks. What method did you use to manage your time?

Presentation: Tell me about a time when you developed a lesson, training, or briefing and presented it to a group.

Problem Solving: Describe a time when you analyzed data to determine multiple solutions to a problem. What steps did you take?

Resource Management: Describe a situation when you capitalized on an employee's skill.

Team Work: Describe a time when you had to deal with a team member who was not pulling his/her weight.

INTERVIEW PREPARATION EXERCISE

Present your best competencies with a great story or example that demonstrates your real behavior.

LEADERSHIP – Inspires, motivates, and guides others toward strategic/operation goals and corporate values. Coaches, mentors, and challenges staff and adapts leadership style to various situations. Consistently demonstrates decisiveness in day-to-day actions. Takes unpopular positions when necessary. Faces adversity head on. Rallies support and strives for consensus to accomplish tasks. Leads by personal example. Demonstrates concern for employees' welfare and safety, by continuously monitoring and eliminating potentially hazardous or unhealthy work situations.

Can you give me an example where you led a team?

CONTEXT:

CHALLENGE:

ACTION:

    1.

    2.

    3.

RESULTS:

Prep for your interview using our free CCAR Accomplishment Builder!
www.resume-place.com/ccar_accomplishment

Federal Staffing Basics— Quick Reference

Contents

FEDERAL HIRING BASICS STEP-BY-STEP

Step 1 ▶ Analyze workforce, Identify deficiency, obtain appropriate approvals to hire/fill vacancy

Step 2 ▶ Identify skill gaps, classify position, determine hiring strategy (i.e., area of consideration, grade level, series, etc.)

Step 3 ▶ Review job description for alignment with agency mission goals and objectives

Step 4 ▶ Conduct job analysis to determine essential KSAs and required competencies

Step 5 ▶ Select Assessment Process (i.e., crediting plan ; interview type; and written test or use of subject matter experts)

Step 6 ▶ Choose ranking method: category ranking (all over a certain score) or rule of three (only highest three scorers)

Step 7 ▶ Draft vacancy announcement with 5-7 relevant questions

Step 8 ▶ Post Announcement (starts OPM 45 day timeframe)

Step 9 ▶ HR specialist reviews applications in agreement with assessment method chosen

Step 10 ▶ HR specialist determines eligibility / qualifications / veterans preference and scores applications

Step 11 ▶ Hiring manager/official reviews applications, conducts interviews of desired candidates, and advises HR of desired selection

Step 12 ▶ HR validates that Merit Principles and Veterans Preference has not been violated and extends job offer

Step 13 ▶ Background investigation is initiated

SUCCESSFUL HIRING IS COMPLETE!

COMPETITIVE SERVICE VS. EXCEPTED SERVICE

You compete for your job against the general public.

- You can earn tenure a.k.a. "status" over time
- Status allows you some hiring benefits
- You cannot be easily fired
- You earn raises according to a formula of time served
- Open jobs must be posted online
- You must compete for the job with the general public

Exceptions are made in hiring; for example, you must be physically fit.

- You cannot earn "status"
- You are hired at-will, more like private industry
- You can earn raises according to performance
- You may be hired or fired for special reasons
- Open jobs do not have to be publicly announced
- You do not have to compete for your job with the general public

Agencies can differ by types of service.

COMPETITIVE SERVICE

EXCEPTED SERVICE
(additional agencies listed on page 26)

Jobs can differ by types of service, even within an agency.

COMPETITIVE SERVICE:
GS-2210 Information Technologist

EXCEPTED SERVICE:
Astronaut

CATEGORY RATING

What Happens to Your Application?

Category rating is the ranking and selection process that is now mandatory under Presidential Memorandum, May 11, 2010. We are currently in a time of transition between the previous point system (rate and rank) and the new category rating system.

Three Buckets of Applicants

All of the applications are evaluated and sorted into three groups, which we like to call buckets.

- **Best Qualified** – This is the <u>only</u> group that will get Referred to the Supervisor.

- **Well-Qualified** – This group will <u>not</u> be referred.

- **Qualified** – This group will <u>not</u> be referred.

Minimum Requirements

All applicants who meet the basic qualification requirements established for the position are ranked by being assigned to the appropriate quality category based upon the job-related assessment tool(s)—the Questionnaire!

"If you're not in the top bucket, you're not in the game!"

– Kathryn Troutman

HOW VETERANS' PREFERENCE IS APPLIED

The following steps demonstrate how veterans' preference is applied in category rating.

1. Applicants are rated.

The following appplicant list was collected from a **U.S. citizen** announcement. Their applications are evaluated and they are given one of three ratings, such as Good, Better, and Best.

2. Veterans' Preference is applied based on veteran's status.

- CPS: disability of 30% or more (10 points)
- CP: disability of at least 10% but less than 30% (10 points)
- TP: served at specific time and not disabled (5 points)
- XP: less than 10% disability or derived preference for certain family members (10 points)

> **Veterans' preference rules apply to vacancy announcements that use category rating to assess candidates and are open to all U.S. citizens. Veterans' preference rules do not apply in internal merit promotion announcements.**

3. CPS and CP rise to the highest quality category.

Qualified preference eligibles with a compensable service-connected disability of 30% or more (CPS) and those with a compensable service-connected disability of more than 10% but less than 30% (CP) are placed at the top of the highest quality category.

In our example below, Dom, who scored good and was originally placed in the "Qualified" category, is move to the "Best Qualified" category based on being a disabled veteran (CP or CPS). Once in the Best Qualified category the selecting official may not select a non-veteran over Dom or Chris (disabled veterans do not have priority of non-disabled vets in category rating).

	Status	Rating	Preference	Bucket
Dom	**Disabled vet**	**Good**	**CP**	**Best Qualified**
Chris	**Non-disabled vet**	**Best**	**TP**	**Best Qualified**
Anne	Non-vet	Best		Best Qualified
Mario	Non-vet	Best		Best Qualified
Sheila	Non-disabled vet	Better	TP	Well Qualified
Betty	Non-vet	Better		Well Qualified
Cory	Non-disabled vet	Good	TP	Qualified
Suzie	Non-vet	Good		Qualified
Aida	Non-vet	Good		Qualified

FEDERAL HIRING PROGRAMS (APPOINTMENTS)

Open to all US Citizens

Known as the "public announcement," veterans' preference applies

Direct Hire — 143

Pathways Internships — 143

Federal Employees with Status and those eligible based on Special Appointment Authority*

Known as the "internal announcement," veterans' preference does not apply

Merit Promotion/Lateral moves for current federal employees

Reinstatement of previous federal employees with status

Veteran's Employment Opportunity Act — 144

Veteran's Recruitment Act — 144

30% or more Disabled Vets — 144

Military Spouse Program (MSP) — 145

Schedule A Person with Disabilities — 146

Non-Competitive Hiring Programs*

No announcement necesary

Veteran's Recruitment Act — 144

30% or More Disabled Veterans — 144

Schedule A Hiring for Individuals with Disabilities — 146

Department of Defense Hiring Programs

Title 21 Dual Status Technician Jobs — 148

Program S for Military Spouses - 149

* NOTE: While not all inclusive, these are the most common special hiring authorities/programs. Other Special Appointing Authorities (i.e., for doctors, lawyers, Peace Corp volunteers, etc.), and Non-competitive Hiring Programs (Interpreters, Assistants for Persons with Disabilities, etc.) can be found in Title 5 of the Code of Federal Regulation.

DIRECT HIRE

Direct hire provides agencies a quick way to hire individuals in the competitive service. Positions filled through direct hire are posted on USAJOBS. Agencies use direct hire authority when there is a shortage of qualified candidates (i.e., an agency is unable to identify qualified candidates despite extensive recruitment or extended announcement periods), or when an agency has a critical hiring need, such as an emergency or unanticipated event, or changed mission requirements. Agencies are allowed to forgo rating and ranking qualified candidates or applying veterans' preference for direct hire.

Certain agencies have direct hire authority for certain occupations. However, OPM allows the government-wide use of direct hire authority for the following occupations:

- Information technology management related to cybersecurity
- Intelligence analyst
- Medical officers, nurses, social workers, and pharmacists
- Contract specialists

PATHWAYS

The Pathways Program offers clear paths to federal internships for students from high school through post-graduate school and to careers for recent graduates, and provides meaningful training and career development opportunities for individuals who are at the beginning of their federal service.

Veterans' preference DOES apply to Pathways announcements.

 Internship Program: This program is for current students enrolled in a wide variety of educational institutions from high school to graduate level, with paid opportunities to work in agencies and explore federal careers while still in school. Additional information about the Internship Program can be found at www.opm.gov/HiringReform/Pathways/program/interns/.

 Recent Graduates Program: This program is for individuals who have recently graduated from qualifying educational institutions or programs and seek a dynamic career development program with training and mentorship. To be eligible, applicants must apply within two years of degree or certificate completion (except for veterans precluded from doing so due to their military service obligation, who will have up to six years to apply). Additional information about the Recent Graduates Program can be found at: www.opm.gov/HiringReform/Pathways/program/graduates/.

 Presidential Management Fellows Program: For more than three decades, the PMF Program has been the federal government's premier leadership development program for advanced degree candidates. This program is now for individuals who have received a qualifying advanced degree within the preceding two years. For complete program information visit: www.pmf.gov.

VETERANS EMPLOYMENT OPPORTUNITIES ACT OF 1998 (VEOA)

What it provides: This gives eligible veterans access to jobs otherwise available only to status employees. Veterans are not accorded preference as a factor but are allowed to compete for job opportunities that are not offered to other external candidates. A VEOA eligible who is selected will be given a career or career-conditional appointment.

When it is used: Agencies may appoint VEOA eligibles who have competed under agency merit promotion announcements when they are recruiting from outside their workforce.

Who is eligible: VEOA eligibility applies to the following categories of veterans:
- Preference eligibles; and
- Service personnel separated after three or more years of continuous active service performed under honorable conditions.

VETERANS RECRUITMENT APPOINTMENT (VRA)

(Formerly Veterans Readjustment Appointment)

What it provides: VRA allows appointment of eligible veterans up to GS-11 or equivalent. Veterans are hired under excepted appointments to positions that are otherwise in the competitive service. After the veteran satisfactorily completes two years of service, the individual must be converted noncompetitively to a career or career-conditional appointment.

When it is used: VRA is used for filling entry-level to mid-level positions.

Who is eligible: VRA eligibility applies to the following veterans:
- Disabled veterans;
- Veterans who served on active duty in the Armed Forces during a war declared by Congress, or in a campaign or expedition for which a campaign badge has been authorized;
- Veterans who, while serving on active duty in the Armed Forces, participated in a military operation for which the Armed Forces Service Medal was awarded; and
- Veterans separated from active duty within three years.

30 PERCENT OR MORE DISABLED VETERANS

What it provides: This authority enables a hiring manager to appoint an eligible candidate to any position for which he or she is qualified, without competition. Unlike the VRA, there's no grade-level limitation. Initial appointments are time-limited appointment of at least 60 days; however, the manager can noncompetitively convert the individual to permanent status at any time during the time-limited appointment.

When it is used: This authority is a good tool for filling positions at any grade level quickly.

Who is eligible: Eligibility applies to the following categories:
- Disabled veterans who were retired from active military service with a disability rating of 30% or more; and
- Disabled veterans rated by the Dept. of Veterans Affairs (VA) (within the preceding year) as having a compensable service-connected disability of 30% or more.

MILITARY SPOUSE EMPLOYMENT PREFERENCE (MSP)

What it provides: MSP provides priority in the employment selection process for military spouses who are relocating as a result of their military spouse's PCS. Spouse preference may be used for most vacant positions in DOD and applies only within the commuting area of the permanent duty station of the sponsor. Spouses may apply for MSP as early as 30 days prior to their reporting date at the new duty station.

When it is used: 1) Placements into competitive civil service vacancies in the 50 states, the Territories, the Possessions, and the District of Columbia; 2) Employment in foreign areas; 3) Nonappropriated Fund (NAF) employment; 4) Non-competitive appointments in the civil service for spouses of certain members of the Armed Forces.

Who is eligible: This preference does not apply to separation or retirement moves. Spouses must be found best qualified for the position and may exercise preference no more than one time per permanent relocation of the sponsor. (If you accept a position with time limitations, i.e., temporary, term, intermittent, or NAF with flexible work schedules, you do not lose your MSP.)

APPOINTMENT OF CERTAIN MILITARY SPOUSES

What it provides: As of 9/11/09, federal agencies were granted the authority to hire "qualified" military spouses using a special appointing authority established through Executive Order 13473. Spouses can find out about job opportunities by going to USAJOBS or websites of specific agencies.

When it is used: The use of this authority is discretionary by federal agencies and the hiring managers. The authority is not limited to specific positions or grade levels, but spouses must meet the same requirements as other applicants, to include qualification requirements. Spouses are not provided any "hiring preference," nor does it create an entitlement to federal jobs over other qualified applicants. It is the applicant's responsibility to apply for a job and request consideration for employment under this authority (Executive Order 13473) as a military spouse.

Who is eligible:
- Spouses of service members serving on PCS for 180 days or more (provided the spouse relocates to the member's new permanent duty station)
- Spouses of retired service members (who retired under Chapter 61, Title 10, USA) with a disability rating of 100% at the time of retirement
- Spouses of former service members who retired or were released and have a 100% disability rating from the VA
- Un-remarried widows or widowers of Armed Forces members killed while serving on active duty.

SCHEDULE A HIRING PROGRAM

Individuals with Disabilities, Including Veterans with a 30% or Greater Service Connected Disability

What it provides: Persons with disabilities (and Wounded Warriors) may apply for both competitive and noncompetitive federal jobs. Jobs that are filled noncompetitively do not have to be advertised. Instead, a selecting official can select a person with a disability who has a Schedule A certification and is qualified for the job. People who are selected for jobs must meet the qualification requirements and be able to perform the essential duties with or without reasonable accommodation.

When it is used: People who are disabled and have a certification letter may apply for noncompetitive appointment through the Schedule A hiring authority. Applicants with certification letters may apply directly to agencies' Selective Placement Program Coordinators or their equivalent to be considered for jobs. Managers as well as individuals with disabilities may contact the agency's Selective Placement Program Coordinator or human resources office or their equivalent to obtain more information about sources for applicants with disabilities.

Who is eligible: For non-competitive Schedule A appointments, a person must have a disability such as an intellectual disability (mental retardation), severe physical disability, or psychiatric disability. The applicant must also obtain a certification letter from a licensed medical professional, licensed vocational rehabilitation specialist, or any government agency (federal, state, or District of Columbia) that issues or provides disability benefits.

Agencies appointing under Schedule A hiring authority will determine whether the individual is likely to succeed in performing the duties of the job in the particular work environment. In some cases the agency may decide to observe the applicant on the job to assess whether he or she is able to perform the duties through a temporary appointment of up to 90 days.

Tips for Veterans Waiting for Disability Rating from Veterans Affairs

Qualifying vets and Wounded Warriors in transition programs can apply for federal jobs through Schedule A, which may be an option for those applying for federal positions who have not yet received their VA disability rating.

Vets can apply for Schedule A certification or to get assistance through the local State Vocational Rehabilitation Program even though they receive their services through the VA program. The State Vocational Rehabilitation Program can get the ball rolling and make connection(s) to the VA program.

For more information:

- Selective Placement Program Coordinator (SPPC) Directory:
  http://apps.opm.gov/sppc_directory/

- OPM training on hiring people with disabilities:
  http://golearn.gov/hiringreform/hpwd/index.htm

Abstracted from http://www.opm.gov/disability/mngr_3-13.asp
Applicable regulation: 5 CFR 213.3102(u)

To receive your Schedule A certification, you will need a letter confirming your disability, unless the disability is obvious, such as missing limbs or impaired mobility.

Who can write the Schedule A certification?

- A licensed medical professional (e.g. a physician or other medical professional certified by a State, the District of Columbia, or a US territory to practice medicine)

- A licensed vocational rehabilitation specialist or any Government agency such as Federal, state, or District of Columbia that issues or provides disability benefits.

- Each agency has the right to decide what documentation it will accept (i.e. licensed audiologist, clinical social worker, etc.)

To Whom It May Concern:

This letter serves as certification that [name of applicant] is an individual with a documented severe disability, and can be considered for employment under the Schedule A hiring authority pursuant to 5 CFR 213.3102(u).

Thank you for your interest in considering this individual for employment.

You may contact me at xxx-xxx-xxxx.

Signed,

[Medical Doctor or Rehabilitation Counselor]

TITLE 32 DUAL STATUS TECHNICIAN JOBS

"Dual status" military technicians are federal civilian employees who are required to maintain military reserve status as a condition of their employment. They are covered by both Title 5 (Civil Service employees) and Title 32 (Technician Act), and are generally required to maintain membership in the National Guard as a condition of their employment.

Military technicians are assigned to civilian positions in administration and training of reserve component units, or in maintaining and repairing reserve component supplies and equipment. They are required to attend weekend drills and annual training with their reserve unit, and can be involuntarily ordered to active duty the same way as other members of the Selected Reserve.

The Department of Defense, the Army, the Air Force, and the National Guard Bureau all oversee dual-status technicians. There are no dual status technicians in the Navy Reserve, Marine Corp Reserve and Coast Guard Reserve. The state Adjutant Generals are the designated employer of dual status military technicians.

Many members of the armed forces start their civilian job search prior to discharge or release from active duty and do not have a DD-214 when applying for federal jobs. The Veterans Opportunity to Work (VOW) Act serves to ensure these individuals do not lose the opportunity to be considered for federal service (and awarded their veterans' preference entitlements if applicable) despite not having a DD-214 to submit along with their resumes. **In lieu of the DD-214, veterans and preference eligibles can submit other written documentation from the Armed Forces certifying that the service member is expected to be discharged or released from active duty service in the Armed Forces under honorable conditions not later than 120 days after the date the certification is signed.**

>> Request a "Statement of Service" from your Administrative Officer stating that you will be separating from the military on a certain date. This way you can apply for federal jobs before you receive your DD-214.

DOD MILITARY SPOUSE PRIORITY PLACEMENT PROGRAM (PPP) / PROGRAM S

MILITARY SPOUSE PREFERENCE PROGRAM (PROGRAM S)
Priority Placement Program Fact Sheet

Military Spouses can find opportunities for DOD positions in the US when on PCS orders with their spouse!

Military spouses who are relocating with their active duty U.S. Armed Forces spouse ("sponsor") as a result of permanent change of station (PCS) orders may be eligible for priority consideration/noncompetitive appointment to competitive service Department of Defense (DOD) positions in the continental U.S., territories, and possessions. The term "Armed Forces" includes active duty Coast Guard and full-time National Guard.

The program does not apply to excepted service positions; positions in foreign overseas areas; positions filled through delegated examining or direct hire authorities; and certain other positions.

Which USAJOBS positions are available for Program S consideration?

Department of Defense positions that are located within driving distance of your spouse's PCS order duty location are available. This program does not apply to non-DOD positions.

Who is eligible?

Spouse preference eligibility begins 30 days prior to the sponsor's reporting date, and continues at the new duty station after relocation. Eligibility continues throughout the tour (with a requirement for re-registration after 12 months) until the spouse accepts or declines a continuing (permanent) appropriated fund position in the commuting area. There is a limit of one permanent appointment per PCS and the spouse must be immediately available for appointment. Until recently, most spouses gained their eligibility through their current or prior service as federal career or career-conditional employees (or by virtue of certain other status).

Where are the positions?

Positions must be within the geographic commuting area of the permanent duty station.

Getting started with Program S Registration

Registration Process Eligible spouses register for Program S at the Civilian Personnel Advisory Center (CPAC) at the sponsor's prior or current duty station. It is important to bring a narrative resume and your most recent performance appraisal. You are also required to present the PCS orders showing authorization to accompany the sponsor to the new duty station, as well as proof of marriage (certificate of marriage or license).

Your resume will be reviewed, scored, and added to the Program S Database

The Human Resources specialists will assess the series and grades for which you are qualified. If you do not have prior federal civilian service, the HR specialist will evaluate your experience, education, and training. It is essential that your resume substantiate your knowledge, skills, and abilities related to the series (1 or more) and grade(s) you are pursuing. See Chapter 10 of the PPP Handbook for information on "occupational codes".

How will your resume be matched against job announcements in USAJOBS?

An HR specialist who is managing USAJOBS announcements will see that you are listed on Program S. This HR person will see a MATCH between the announcement and your registration in Program S. The HR specialist will contact you about the position and will either tell you to apply or just notify you of the match.

What happens when you apply and you are Best Qualified for the position for a matched Program S + USAJOBS announcement?

You will apply for the position, and if you are Best Qualified for the position based on your resume and the questionnaire answers, you will be considered for the position. Except for those having a higher priority, a better qualified military spouse "blocks the selection of other competitive candidates."

What about Veterans' Preference and Program S Applications?

If you are applying to an internal job announcement, veterans' preference will not be considered the same way as it would be for a U.S. citizen announcement. Your resume could rise above a veteran's due to Program S registration.

For more information

- DOD PPP Handbook, read Chapter 14 for Military Spouse PPP:
  www.cpms.osd.mil/Content/Documents/PPPHandbookAug2012(2).pdf

- To review program specifics eligibility, see Chapter 14 of the Department of Defense Priority Placement Program (PPP) Handbook:
  www.cpms.osd.mil/Content/Documents/PPPHandbookAug2012%282%29.pdf

- Military Spouse Program S Fact Sheet:
  www.cpms.osd.mil/Content/Documents/PPP-Program%20S.pdf

Program S registration codes for our military spouse case study, Bobbi Robins:

-- EXPERIENCE --		FROM		TO	TITLE	
		201402		201504	EMPLOYMENT SERVICES & TRNG CTR	
		200911		201302	FAMILY READINESS OFFICER	
-- SKILLS --	PG	SER	HI	LO	EX	HD
	GS	0101	09	09		
		Options:EAP FSP				
	GS	0186	07	07		
		Options:NOA				
	GS	0301	09	09		
		Options:FSP NOA				
	GS	0303	07	07		
		Options:FSP				

INDEX

INDEX CONT.

ABOUT THE AUTHOR: KATHRYN TROUTMAN

1. Founder, President, and Manager of The Resume Place®, the first federal job search consulting and federal resume writing service in the world, and the producer of www.resume-place.com, the first website devoted to federal resume writing.

2. Pioneer designer of the federal resume format in 1995 with the publication of the leading resource for federal Human Resources and jobseekers worldwide— the *Federal Resume Guidebook*.

3. Developer of the Ten Steps to a Federal Job®, a licensed curriculum and turnkey training program taught by more than 2,000 Certified Federal Job Search Trainers™ (CFJST) around the world.

4. Leading Federal Resume Writing, KSA, Resumix, ECQ and Federal Interview government contracted trainer. GSA Schedule Holder.

5. Author of numerous federal career publications (in addition to the *Federal Resume Guidebook* mentioned above):

The *Military to Federal Career Guide* is the first book for military personnel and is now in its 2nd edition, featuring veteran federal resumes. Troutman recognized the need for returning military personnel from Iraq, Afghanistan, and Kosovo to have a resource available to them in their searches for government jobs.

Ten Steps to a Federal Job was published two months after 9/11 and was written for private industry jobseekers seeking first-time positions in the federal government, where they could contribute to our nation's security. Now in its third edition.

The *Jobseeker's Guide* started initially as the companion course handout to the *Ten Steps* book, but captured its own following when it became the handout text used by over 200 military installations throughout the world for transitioning military and family members. Now in its seventh edition.

With the looming human capital crisis and baby boomers retiring in government, the *Student's Federal Career Guide* was co-authored with Kathryn's daughter and MPP graduate, Emily Troutman, and is the first book for students pursuing a federal job. Now in its third edition, including the latest information on the changing structure of student programs, plus additional guidance for veterans taking advantage of the Post-9/11 GI Bill.

Resumes for Dummies by Joyce Lain Kennedy is renowned as the premier guidebook for resume writing. Kathryn and The Resume Place staff served as designers and producers of all the private industry resume samples for the fifth edition.

OTHER CONTRIBUTORS

Charles Clark

Human Resources Consultant; Prior Federal Human Resources Manager; Air Force Veteran; Certified Federal Career Job Search Trainer and Career Coach

Charles Clark has over 29 years of Human Resources experience, with 15+ years in Human Resource Management.

While with the U.S. Census Bureau, Charles served in multiple capacities, all with a focus on federal staffing, strategic recruitment, and special hiring authorities. He served as Chief of Diversity and Inclusion, Disability Programs Manager, and Acting Chief, Strategic Recruitment and Outreach Branch. His responsibilities included establishing strategic diversity recruitment policies, ensuring adherence to federal staffing regulations, analyzing skills and qualifications, reasonable accommodations programs for individuals with disabilities, and the selective placement program for hiring veterans and persons with disabilities.

Prior to joining the federal government, Charles completed a military career with the U.S. Air Force, culminating as the Superintendent of the Air Force District of Washington's Manpower, Personnel and Services Directorate. Additionally, Charles served as the DoD Presidential Support Program Manager and Senior Enlisted Advisor to the Executive Secretary for the Department of Defense.

Charles' extensive knowledge and experience provides him keen insight into the complex hiring polices of the federal government. He uses this knowledge to assist individuals to obtain federal employment and has been very successful; he has a particular focus on assisting veterans and individuals with disabilities in their efforts to join the federal workforce.

Charles provides federal HR staffing consultation and education services for The Resume Place, and serves as an Instructor for the Federal Career Training Institute. As an FCTI instructor, Charles has provided federal staffing training to numerous University Career Counselors, Military Transition and Employment Specialists, Vocational Rehab Counselors, and State Employment Agency Representatives, leading to their certification as Federal Job Search Trainers and Career Coaches.

Paulina Chen

Designer & Developmental Editor

Paulina was working at the U.S. Environmental Protection Agency when Kathryn came to the EPA to provide federal resume consultations. Kathryn noticed Paulina's ability to communicate complex information in a straightforward, easy-to-understand way. Kathryn offered Paulina her first freelance opportunity—to design and lay out the interior pages for the first edition of *Ten Steps to a Federal Job*. Now many years later, this team is still collaborating, and the *Jobseeker's Guide 7th Edition* is their fourteenth book project together. Paulina also assists The Resume Place and the Federal Career Training Institute with their websites and marketing efforts and is a Certified Federal Job Search Trainer.

VETERAN FEDERAL CAREER CONSULTING AND RESUME WRITING SERVICES

We have trained writers who specialize in translating military experience into skills and qualifications for federal positions. We can help you with an outstanding federal resume that can get you referred to a supervisor.

We are pleased to offer America's veterans the following:

- Veteran career consultation, full service federal resumes, and cover letters

The Resume Place Resume writers and editors will:

- Review resumes drafted by the veteran
- Determine or confirm best occupational series and grade for the veteran
- Ensure that One Year Specialized Experience is evident for the target positions
- Edit and feature improved keywords for an announcement or classification standard
- Review or confirm accomplishments
- Review and improve format and content
- Finalize the resume in Outline Format with keywords and accomplishments

Get help applying for federal jobs with USAJOBS:

- USAJOBS account and builder setup
- Document uploads, including veterans' documents, transcripts, cover letter, evaluations
- Questionnaire review and completion
- Submission and tracking & follow-up lessons
- Announcement review for next announcements and job search strategies

Check out these useful websites:

- *Free Federal Resume Builder, KSA Builder, Cover Letter Builder and Application Writing Builders*
  www.resume-place.com/resources

- *VetFedJobs*
  vetfedjobs.org

- *Feds Hire Vets*
  www.fedshirevets.gov

- *Mil2FedJobs (State of Maryland)*
  www.dllr.state.md.us/mil2fedjobs

The Resume Place, Inc.
www.resume-place.com
888-480-8265

PUBLICATIONS BY THE RESUME PLACE

Order online at www.resume-place.com | Bulk Orders: (888) 480 8265
FREE SHIPPING of bulk orders in the domestic US and APO; shipping is calculated for HI and overseas

EBooks Available for Immediate Download

Many of our titles are available in PDF or Kindle versions for immediate download from our training site.
Go to www.fedjobtraining.com/ebooks/ebooks-1 and start reading your copy today!

Jobseeker's Guide, 7th Edition

Military to Federal Career Transition Resource
Workbook and guide for the Ten Steps to a Federal Job® training curriculum. Federal job search strategies for first-time jobseekers who are separating military and family members. *$14.95 ea., Bulk Rates Available*

Ten Steps to a Federal Job, 3rd Ed.

Written for a first-time applicant, particularly those making a career change from private industry to federal government. Case studies include 24 before & after successful resumes! *$18.95 ea., Bulk Rates Available*

Federal Resume Guidebook, 6th Ed.

The ultimate guide in federal resume, KSA, and ECQ writing. 30+ samples on the CD-ROM. Easy to use as a template for writing. Specialty occupational series chapters. *$15.95 ea., Bulk Rates Available*

The New SES Application

The SES job application is complex. The New SES Application breaks it down into a step-by-step process based on a popular workshop taught for over 10 years. Plus, the book has updated the SES info to help you navigate hiring reforms currently impacting the Senior Executive Service. *$21.95 ea., Bulk Rates Available*

Military to Federal Career Guide, 2nd Ed.

Federal Resume Writing for Veterans
All samples and insight for military to federal transition for veterans. Samples are in the Outline Format with keywords, accomplishments from military careers. *$14.95 ea., Bulk Rates Available*

Student's Federal Career Guide, 3rd Ed.

3rd Edition takes the 2013 IndieFab Gold Winner for Career Books! Outstanding book for jobseekers who are just getting out of college and whose education will help the applicant get qualified for a position. 20 samples of recent graduate resumes with emphasis on college degrees, courses, major papers, internships, and relevant work experiences. Outstanding usability of samples on the CD-ROM. *$14.95 ea., Bulk Rates Available*

Creating Your First Resume

Creating Your First Resume is a book that will be used at high school and technical school programs nationwide. The new edition boasts brand new resume samples that represent the push toward STEM technical programs to provide training and certifications for high school students. *$8.95 ea.*

Online Federal Resume Database

This Online Federal Resume Database contains more than 110 resume samples and federal job search resources from the current Resume Place publications. Each CD-ROM has a clearly organized interface. Sample resumes are available in Word and PDF format for quick previewing and easy editing. *Individual and Agency / Base Licenses Available*

TEN STEPS TO A FEDERAL JOB® CERTIFICATION PROGRAM

Since 1992, over 2,000 career professionals have benefited from our unique certification in the Ten Steps to a Federal Job® curriculum, and the program continues to grow each year. Get certified and licensed to teach Kathryn Troutman's popular, proven, turnkey curriculum: Ten Steps to a Federal Job® and Federal Resume & KSA Writing curriculum. This course was developed by Kathryn Troutman as a direct result of her training experiences at hundreds of federal agencies throughout the world.

Our three-day program is pre-approved to fulfill 24 continuing education hours for the Center of Credentialing and Education's Global Career Development Facilitator (GCDF) certification.

A few of our 2014 classes

Registration Benefits - Incredible Value!

- Free Multi-User License to Access Our Ten Steps Online Resources (three months)
- Online Federal Resume Database
- Ten Steps eLearning Program
- Federal Career Books for Your Library:
  ◊ *Federal Resume Guidebook*
  ◊ *Jobseeker's Guide*
  ◊ *Ten Steps to a Federal Job*
  ◊ *Military to Federal Career Guide*
  ◊ *Student's Federal Career Guide*
  ◊ *Creating Your First Resume*
  ◊ Beautiful Ten Steps bag
- PowerPoint Presentations for your use as a trainer:
  ◊ Ten Steps to a Federal Job® – Licensed for three years
  ◊ Federal Hiring Program
  ◊ Veteran's and Spouse Hiring Programs
  ◊ Student Federal Hiring Programs

"I just wanted to let you know that attendance at the three-day course in March [2012] has done wonders for my confidence and wonders for my clients. When we go through the OPM Job Factors and the Grading of GS positions, most clients are over-joyed to have opened the "treasure chest" where the mystery of pursuing a Federal Job Position is solved. Thank you for all that you do!! I love the books and find something new EVERY day that I can share with my fellow coaches."

More Information and Registration
www.fedjobtraining.com/certification-programs.htm